Blackstone's Guide to the

DATA PROTECTION ACT 1998

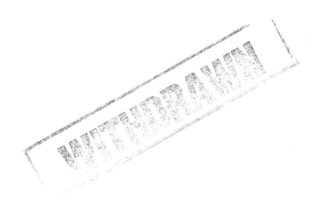

Blackstone's Guide to the

DATA PROTECTION ACT 1998

Peter Carey, LLB, LLM, Solicitor

BLACKSTONE
PRESS LIMITED

First published in Great Britain 1998 by Blackstone Press Limited,
Aldine Place, London W12 8AA. Telephone 0181-740 2277

© P. W. Carey, 1998

ISBN: 1 85431 866 7

British Library Cataloguing in Publication Data
A CIP catalogue record for this book is available from the British Library.

Typeset by Montage Studios Limited, Horsmonden, Kent
Printed by Ashford Colour Press, Gosport, Hants

Contents

Need for data protection — Data Protection Act 1984 — General provisions — Data protection principles — Data Protection Directive

Introduction — Initial definitions — Basic rights of access — *Automated decisions — Identifying other individuals — Multiple requests — Amendments to data — Credit reference agencies — Court order — Transitional exemption* — Preventing processing: general — *Court order — Transitional exemption* — Preventing processing: direct marketing — *Transitional exemption* — Automated decision-taking — *Court order — Exempt decisions — Transitional exemption* — Rectification, blocking, erasure and destruction — *Transitional exemption* — Compensation — *Transitional exemption* — Transitional rights

Introduction — First principle — *Obtaining data — Information to be supplied to the data subject — Presumption of fairness — Tribunal precedent — Criteria for lawful processing — Sensitive personal data — General identifiers* — Am I processing data fairly? — Second principle — Third principle — Fourth principle — Fifth principle — Sixth principle — Seventh principle — *Data processors* — Eighth principle — *Transitional provisions — Exemptions* — Am I transferring data in contravention of the eighth principle?

Introduction — Prohibition on processing — Required information — Exemption from notification — The register — *Public inspection* — Notification of changes — *Criminal offence* — Assessable processing — *Criminal offence* — Data protection supervisors — Duty of disclosure — *Criminal offence* — Do I need to notify?

Preface

The United Kingdom was required to pass the Data Protection Act 1998 as part of its European Union obligations under the Data Protection Directive (95/46/EC). The motivation behind the Directive was a desire to promote personal data privacy rights and to harmonise the data protection laws of Member States.

The Act was passed on 16 July 1998. However, most of the Act's provisions did not come into force at that time. One of the critical dates for compliance with the new provisions was 24 October 1998, which was also the date by which Member States were obliged to implement the Directive. Many of the Act's transitional provisions operate by reference to that date. Any new databases created after 23 October 1998 cannot benefit from the Act's transitional exemptions.

The Data Protection Act 1998 replaces the Data Protection Act 1984 but takes matters somewhat further. Those who are familiar with the old Act will find some common terminology in the new Act but many of the definitions have changed. The definition of 'data' has been widened to incorporate certain manual records and 'processing' now includes virtually anything that can be done with data, including merely reading it on a computer screen. There are new rights of acess to personal data and to be informed of the logic behind automated decision-taking. A data subject is now entitled to know the data controller's source of personal data and may object to (and require the cessation of) certain kinds of processing. There is a new ban, subject to exceptions, on the transfer of personal data to countries other than those which are members of the European Economic Area.

This Guide follows the sequence of the Act in terms of the material it covers, except where deviation is helpful to comprehension. After a brief analysis of data protection laws from a historical perspective (chapter 1), the second chapter considers the rights of data subjects under the new provisions. Chapter 3 looks at the data protection principles including case law under the old Act which is still expected to be relevant. The fourth chapter looks at the notification procedure in terms of the responsibilities of the data controller and the corresponding duties of the Data Protection Commissioner. Chapter 5 is divided into two parts: part 1 looks at permanent exemptions from certain provisions of the Act for particular types of data; part 2 considers transitional exemptions (which are available either until 23 October 2001 or 23 October 2007). The sixth chapter looks at the enforcement regime and considers the purpose of information, special information and enforcement notices. Chapter 7 deals with the criminal offences created by the Act and chapter 8 with transitional provisions generally.

This book is designed to be a comprehensive guide to the provisions of the new Act. It is written from a standpoint which assumes no knowledge of data protection legislation. Those who have worked with the Data Protection Act 1984 will find much that is familiar and I have tried to incorporate references to the old law where I have considered this to be useful.

All references to section or schedule numbers are to the 1998 Act unless otherwise stated. The Data Protection Act 1984 may be referred to as 'the old Act' or 'the 1984 Act'. I have attempted to use 'him' and 'her', and 'he' and 'she' interchangeably wherever possible. All references to one gender should be taken as including the other. The Data Protection Commissioner at the time of writing is female and so will be referred to by using the female gender.

Peter Carey
The College of Law

Acknowledgements

Thanks firstly to Dr Nigel Savage, for suggesting that I write this book. His work (together with Chris Edwards) on the Data Protection Act 1984 will be familiar reading to most of those involved with data protection work in the last few years. Whilst very little of the Savage and Edwards *Guide to the Data Protection Act 1984* is used here, it proved to be essential background information. Many thanks therefore both to Nigel Savage and Chris Edwards for the background material.

Thanks to Rachel Tyack of the College of Law for help with original research, to Robert Wood of Bevan Ashford Solicitors (Exeter) for proofreading and other advice on content and to Sally Paul of Thomson Snell and Passmore (Tunbridge Wells) for technical help with the construction of diagrams.

Special thanks to Elaine Fletcher of the Office of the Data Protection Commissioner for her insights and advice, and to Shelagh Gaskill of Masons Solicitors for invaluable help and guidance on the practical application of the new Act.

Lastly, special thanks to Sasha for her unending support and encouragement.

Chapter 1
Historical Background

NEED FOR DATA PROTECTION

The desirability of data protection legislation arose out of the growing use of computers in the 1970s and the threat to personal privacy that rapid manipulation of data potentially posed. The existing law at that time (which consisted of not much more than a possible action in breach of confidence) was insufficient to deal with concerns about the amount of information relating to individuals which is held by organisations. In the early 1970s the Younger Committee on Privacy (Cmnd 5012, 1972) recommended 10 guiding principles for the use of computers which manipulated personal data:

(a) Information should be regarded as held for a specific purpose and should not be used, without appropriate authorisation, for other purposes.

(b) Access to information should be confined to those authorised to have it for the purpose for which it was supplied.

(c) The amount of information collected and held should be the minimum necessary for the achievement of a specified purpose.

(d) In computerised systems handling information for statistical purposes, adequate provision should be made in their design and programs for separating identities from the rest of the data.

(e) There should be arrangements whereby a subject can be told about the information held concerning him.

(f) The level of security to be achieved by a system should be specified in advance by the user and should include precautions against the deliberate abuse or misuse of information.

(g) A monitoring system should be provided to facilitate the detection of any violation of the security system.

(h) In the design of information systems, periods should be specified beyond which the information should not be retained.

(i) Data held should be accurate. There should be machinery for the correction of inaccuracy and the updating of information.

(j) Care should be taken in coding value judgments.

The government's response to the Younger Report was to publish a White Paper (Cmnd 6353, 1975). In it the government stated that: 'the time has come when those who use computers to handle personal information, however responsible they are, can no longer remain the sole judges of whether their own systems, adequately safeguard privacy' (para. 30). The threat to privacy was identified by the White Paper as arising from five particular features or characteristics of computer operations:

(a)   They facilitate the maintenance of extensive record systems and retention of data in those systems.

(b)   They can make data easily and quickly accessible from many different points.

(c)   They make it possible for data to be transferred quickly from one information system to another.

(d)   They make it possible for data to be combined in ways which might not otherwise be practicable.

(e)   The data are stored, processed and often transmitted in a form which is not directly intelligible.

The remit of the Younger Committee had been to consider whether legislation was needed to 'give further protection to the individual citizen and to commercial and industrial interests against intrusion into privacy by private persons and organisations' and the committee was therefore concerned more with privacy than with data protection as such. Although the proposals of the Younger Committee were never enacted, the government subsequently set up the Lindop Committee to obtain detailed advice on the setting up and composition of a Data Protection Authority. Paragraph 2.04 of the Lindop Committee's report (Cmnd 7341, 1978) stated:

The Younger Committee had to deal with the whole field of privacy. Our task has been to deal with that of data protection. In fact, the two fields overlap, and the area of overlap can be called 'information privacy' or, better, 'data privacy'. It is an important area, and we have a good deal to say about it in this report. But it is not by itself the whole field of data protection, and we have had to consider some matters which do not directly raise questions of privacy. However, we found it useful to examine the concept of data privacy, and its implications and consequences. For this purpose we have used the term data privacy to mean the individual's claim to control the circulation of data about himself.

The Lindop Report went on to recommend the establishment of a Data Protection Authority and Codes of Practice particular to different sectors of the business community. These proposals were not ultimately acted on.

It was the Council of Europe Convention of 1981 that provided the impetus for the passage of the Data Protection Act 1984, the provisions of which correspond more closely with the Convention than with the Lindop Report (in fact the Convention had, at least in part, been based on Sir Kenneth Younger's Report). The most compelling reason for this was the desire of Parliament to conform to an internationally agreed standard for data protection. Without such provision the UK was likely to be excluded from a new elite club of countries which provided for a basic level of protection for individuals and prohibited transborder data flows to non-members.

DATA PROTECTION ACT 1984

General provisions

The 1984 Act introduced a new regime for the holding and processing of 'information recorded in a form in which it can be processed by equipment operating automatically in response to instructions given for that purpose' (data). For the first time, data users — those persons who hold data — were obliged to register with the office of the Data Protection Registrar (DPR). The Act introduced criminal offences for failing to comply with its provisions and a system of compensation for individuals who were caused damage by non-compliance.

The requirement to register with the DPR arose where a data user automatically processed personal data (information which relates to a living individual who can be identified from the information, including any expression of opinion about the individual). The registration form requested the following details:

(a)   the name and address of the data user;
(b)   a description of the personal data held and a statement of the purposes for which the data are held;
(c)   a description of the sources from which the data are obtained, and persons to whom they may be disclosed;
(d)   a list of the countries to which any data may be transferred;
(e)   an address for the receipt of requests from data subjects for access.

Once the Registrar was satisfied with the application, it was entered on the Register, which is open to public inspection (both at the premises of the DPR and also at their Web site: http://www.open.gov.uk/dpr/dprhome.htm). A person carrying on a computer bureau needed only to register his name and address. A data user who processed personal data without being registered committed a criminal offence.

A data subject had the right to request access to any personal data that a data user held on him or her (a small fee was chargeable) and the data user was obliged to supply the information within 40 days of the request. The request could be enforced by the DPR or in the courts.

A data subject who suffered damage which was directly attributable to the inaccuracy, loss or unauthorised disclosure of data, could claim compensation from the data user. This right was enforceable in the courts. A further enforceable right of the data subject was to have any erroneous information held by the data user rectified or erased.

Data protection principles

The regime under the 1984 Act was underpinned by certain fundamental principles, which were originally set out in the Convention. The legislation adopted the Continental model by expressing the eight principles in very general terms. For this reason they were not enforceable through the courts but only by the DPR and the Data Protection Tribunal. The principles, with one exception, were not dissimilar to those now contained in the 1998 Act, and were as follows:

1.   The information to be contained in personal data shall be obtained, and personal data shall be processed, fairly and lawfully.
2.   Personal data shall be held only for one or more specified and lawful purposes.
3.   Personal data held for any purpose or purposes shall not be used or disclosed in any manner incompatible with that purpose or those purposes.
4.   Personal data held for any purpose or purposes shall be adequate, relevant and not excessive in relation to that purpose or those purposes.
5.   Personal data shall be accurate and, where necessary, kept up to date.
6.   Personal data held for any purpose or purposes shall not be kept for longer than is necessary for that purpose or those purposes.
7.   An individual shall be entitled—
    (a)   at reasonable intervals and without undue delay or expense—
      (i)   to be informed by any data user whether he holds personal data of which that individual is the subject; and
      (ii)   to access to any such data held by a data user; and
    (b)   where appropriate, to have such data corrected or erased.
8.   Appropriate security measures shall be taken against unauthorised access to, or alteration, disclosure or destruction of, personal data and against accidental loss or destruction of personal data.

Although the principles formed the backbone of the 1984 data protection legislation there was no requirement as such to comply with their provisions. There were however potential consequences for non-compliance, such as, for example, the service of an enforcement notice.

DATA PROTECTION DIRECTIVE

The European Data Protection Directive on the protection of individuals with regard to the processing of personal data and on the free movement of such data (95/46/EC) required implementation in Member States by 24 October 1998. It is a general framework legislative provision which has as its aims:

    (a)   the protection of an individual's privacy in relation to the processing of personal data;
    (b)   the harmonisation of data protection laws of the Member States.

It sets out the conditions under which the processing of personal data is lawful, the rights of data subjects and the standards of data quality. The Directive seeks to establish an equivalent level of protection for personal data in all Member States, so as to facilitate the transfer of personal data across national boundaries in the European Union.

The Directive applies to personal data processed wholly or partly by automatic means, and to manual data held in filing systems structured by reference to individuals, but it does not apply to activities which fall outside the scope of EU law. It excludes areas within Titles V and VI of the Treaty on European Union, public safety, defence, State security (including the economic well-being of the State when the processing relates to State security matters) and the activities of the State in areas of criminal law. It also specifically excludes domestic or household activities.

Article 6 establishes fundamental principles which have to be respected when personal data are processed. These principles are superficially similar to those in the 1984 Act. Article 7 sets out a number of conditions which must be satisfied before data can be processed. Data processing must be with the data subject's consent except when processing is necessary:

(a)   for the performance of a contract to which the data subject is party;
(b)   for compliance with a legal obligation;
(c)   to protect the vital interests of the data subject;
(d)   to perform a task carried out in the public interest or in the exercise of official authority; or
(e)   to meet the legitimate interests of the data controller, unless those interests are overridden by the interests or fundamental rights and freedoms of the data subject.

Certain special categories of data which reveal information about a person's racial or ethnic origin, political opinions, religious or philosophical beliefs, trade union membership, health or sex life, and data concerning offences and criminal convictions, may be processed only under certain strict conditions. One of these is the explicit consent of the data subject (except where the Member States' laws provide that the prohibition on sensitive processing cannot be waived by the data subject giving his or her consent).

The data subject has the right to be informed, where data are collected either from the data subject or from a third party, of the identity of the data controller, the purposes for which the data are used, and of any further information which is necessary to ensure fair processing.

Other rights include:

(a)   the right of access to personal data without constraint, at reasonable intervals and without excessive delays or expense;
(b)   the right to have incomplete or inaccurate data rectified, erased or blocked;
(c)   the right to object to processing of personal data, and where there is a justified objection, to have the processing stopped;
(d)   the right to object to personal data being used for purposes of direct marketing;
(e)   the right not to be subject to a decision that has legal effects and which is based solely on automated processing of data (unless the decision is in connection with a contract where the results do not adversely affect the data subject, or is authorised by law and provided that the data subject's interests are safeguarded).

Data security must be such as to ensure that personal data are protected against accidental or unlawful destruction or accidental loss. Data must also be protected against unauthorised alteration, disclosure or access and all other forms of unlawful processing. The level of security must be appropriate to the risks represented by the processing and the nature of the data to be protected, having regard to the state of technology and cost.

The Directive sets out the conditions under which personal data which are being processed or which are intended for processing may be transferred to countries outside the European Union. In general, a transfer may only take place if the third country ensures an adequate level of protection for the rights and freedoms of data subjects. There are certain exceptions, for example, if the data subject gives consent or if the transfer is necessary or legally required on public interest grounds.

Each Member State is required to set up a supervisory authority to oversee the application in its country of the national provisions giving effect to the Directive. Computerised processing operations must be notified to and registered by the supervisory authority. It is for Member States to decide whether or not to apply these requirements to manual data. There is provision for exemption from or simplification of the notification requirements in certain cases.

Member States were required to bring the Directive into force before 24 October 1998. Following successful representations from the UK a provision was included in the Directive which allowed Member States to provide a derogation in relation to the processing of data already held in manual filing systems when the national provisions came into force. However, such filing systems must be made to comply with the provisions of the Directive before the expiry of 12 years from the date when it was adopted, i.e., by 24 October 2007.

Member States are required to provide adequate legal redress (including compensation for damage) for breach of the provisions of the Directive.

Chapter 2
Rights of Individuals

INTRODUCTION

Chapter 1 shows how the historical development of data protection legislation is founded in a concern for the individual's right to privacy. It is fitting therefore that the first substantive chapter of this book should deal with the rights that an individual is given under the Data Protection Act 1998. In many cases they are considerably stronger than the equivalent rights conferred under the Data Protection Act 1984.

The basic rights of the individual are contained in part II of the 1998 Act, but in order to analyse them it will be necessary first to define some terminology, much of which is contained in part I. The last section of this chapter discusses certain transitional rights which are available until 23 October 2007.

The individual's rights are subject to certain exemptions enacted for the benefit of data controllers. The rights in this chapter should therefore be considered in conjunction with chapter 5.

INITIAL DEFINITIONS

For the purposes of the legislation the person who is protected is called the 'data subject'. The definition of data subject has not changed from the previous legislation and thus remains 'an individual who is the subject of personal data'.

Section 1(1) defines 'data' as:

information which—

(a) is being processed by means of equipment operating automatically in response to instructions given for that purpose,

(b) is recorded with the intention that it should be processed by means of such equipment,

(c) is recorded as part of a relevant filing system or with the intention that it should form part of a relevant filing system, or

(d) does not fall within paragraph (a), (b) or (c) but forms part of an accessible record [i.e., a health record (see below), an educational record (Schedule 11) or an accessible public record (Schedule 12)].

The 1984 Act related only to automatically processed data. The right of access to material that forms part of a relevant filing system (and therefore to paper-based records) in the 1998 Act is likely, for UK businesses, to be the most costly and time-consuming aspect of the new regime. Material forming part of a relevant filing system immediately before 24 October 1998 did not need to comply with the provisions of the Act before that date. The application of the Act to 'existing' processing of such data after that date is subject to the statute's transitional provisions — see chapter 5, part 2 and chapter 8. A 'relevant filing system' is defined (s. 1(1)) as:

> any set of information relating to individuals to the extent that, although the information is not processed by means of equipment operating automatically in response to instructions given for that purpose, the set is structured, either by reference to individuals or by reference to criteria relating to individuals, in such a way that specific information relating to a particular individual is readily accessible.

There is likely to be considerable controversy over precisely what is included within this definition. It seems that the key characteristics of a relevant filing system will be the structuring by reference to individuals and/or the ready accessibility of specific information. A set of manual personnel files, each relating individually to a specific employee, could well fall within the definition. So too could a card-index filing system. However the Government has expressed some concern over the impact of the new legislation on small to medium sized enterprises, particularly in respect of the fact that the most likely manual files that such enterprises hold are personnel files. It could be argued that a personnel file in which everything is inserted merely in date order will not be structured in such a way that the internal contents of the files will be readily accessible. Such files will therefore not be caught by the Act. On the other hand where personnel files contain proformas or internal structuring so that there is e.g., a section for attendance at work, a section for training courses taken and a section for professional qualifications gained, then this will be a file which contains an internal structure which renders the information readily accessible.

A single ring binder containing an individual's personal data may not be a structured file, and therefore would not form part of a relevant filing system. It is unlikely that an unstructured collection of papers which only incidentally contain personal data would be caught by the provisions. If manually recorded data do not form part of a relevant filing system then there is no need to comply with any of the provisions in the Act so far as that data is concerned.

The information that gives rise to the rights of the data subject is called 'personal data' and is defined in s. 1(1) as:

> data which relate to a living individual who can be identified—
> (a)   from those data, or
> (b)   from those data and other information which is in the possession of, or is likely to come into the possession of, the data controller.

Personal data includes 'any *expression of opinion* about the individual and any *indication of the intentions* of the data controller or any other person in respect of the individual' (emphasis added). This clearly has personnel or human resources implications for employers — a manager's statement of intentions concerning an employee's promotion or demotion or the manager's opinion of an employee is within the definition. Certain statements of opinion by way of reference are exempt from certain of the provisions of the Act, as are records of intention in relation to negotiations and personal data processed for the purpose of management forecasting or planning — see chapter 5, part 1.

Where a data controller possesses two databases then, provided an individual can be identified from the information in both together, the relevant content of each amounts to personal data. This is true even if the individual cannot be identified from one of the sources alone. If personal data are contained in an encrypted database and the data controller possesses (or is likely to possess at some time) the key for decryption then the encrypted data and the key together amount to personal data. The definition of personal data in the 1998 Act goes further than its predecessor by applying not only to information in the possession of the data controller, but also to information likely to come into the controller's possession. The Directive went even further by not including the words 'likely to come into the possession of', thus rendering an encrypted database personal data where the key existed anywhere in the world, however unlikely it was that the key would have come into the possession of the data controller. It is not clear how 'likely' will be construed.

A 'data controller' is 'a person who (either alone or jointly or in common with other persons) determines the purposes for which and the manner in which any personal data are, or are to be, processed' (s. 1(1)). This is a wider definition than the corresponding 'data user' under the 1984 Act and means that there may be more than one data controller per piece of information.

'Processing', in relation to information or data, means:

obtaining, recording or holding the information or data or carrying out any operation or set of operations on the information or data, including—
    (a)   organisation, adaptation or alteration of the information or data,
    (b)   retrieval, consultation or use of the information or data,
    (c)   disclosure of the information or data by transmission, dissemination or otherwise making available, or
    (d)   alignment, combination, blocking, erasure or destruction of the information or data.

This definition of processing is very much wider than in the previous statute, and it is the belief of the first Data Protection Commissioner, Elizabeth France, that the concept of processing is possibly without limit and could include anything that can be done with data. It certainly covers such things as opening and reading a manual file and even extends to merely calling up or reading a piece of information on a computer screen.

Example 1

Postal Ordering Services Ltd advertises kitchen and bathroom products in a national newspaper. Fiona sees the advertisement and telephones the company for a brochure. She gives her name, address, telephone number and date of birth. The telephone operator enters this information into the company's computer database as Fiona is speaking. The terminology of the 1998 Act applies as follows:

Data controller	Postal Ordering Services Ltd.
Data subject	Fiona.
Personal data	information about Fiona's name, address, telephone number and date of birth.
Processing	this occurs where the personal data is: requested from Fiona; entered into the computer system; read on-screen; printed out; used to send a brochure.

Example 2

Caroline is employed by Safe Banking plc, a high-street bank. The personnel department holds payroll details on computer, and other records in written form. The written records are held in files sorted alphabetically by employee surname and contain details such as length of employment and staff and appraisal matters. They also contain line managers' recommendations for promotion. Safe Banking plc is the data controller. Caroline is the data subject. All the details concerning Caroline which are held on computer and in the personnel files are personal data. Any reading, alteration, copying, addition to, disclosure or transfer of that data will amount to processing for the purposes of the Act.

BASIC RIGHTS OF ACCESS

Section 7 of the 1998 Act provides that a data subject is entitled, upon written request to a data controller, to be promptly informed whether personal data of which the individual is the data subject are being processed by or on behalf of the data controller. A fee (subject to the statutory maximum — currently £10) may be charged by the data controller for this service and the data controller has 40 days (or such other period as may be prescribed) from the receipt by the data controller of such a request to comply. The 40-day time limit does not start to run until the data controller has received the fee and/or has been supplied with sufficient information to enable compliance with the request. A request for information need not be complied with if the data controller has received insufficient information to be satisfied as to the identity of the person making the request. The Secretary of State may prescribe circumstances where a fee is not chargeable.

Where personal data are being processed by or on behalf of the data controller the data subject is entitled to be given a description of:

(a) the personal data of which that individual is the data subject,
(b) the purposes for which they are being or are to be processed, and
(c) the recipients or classes of recipients to whom they are or may be disclosed.

In addition the data subject is entitled to have communicated to him or her *in a form which is capable of being understood*:

(a) the information constituting any personal data of which that individual is the data subject, and
(b) any information available to the data controller as to the source of those data.

In most cases the first of these rights of the data subject will be met by the data controller forwarding to the data subject a copy of the information (plus an intelligible explanation of its content where the meaning is obscure because, for example, codes or abbreviations have been used). Indeed, s. 8 contains an obligation to 'supply a copy in permanent form' unless:

(a)   the supply of such a copy is not possible or would involve disproportionate effort, or
(b)   the data subject waives this right.

The right to receive information as to the source of the data is a new right that did not appear in the 1984 legislation. Data controllers who are concerned about disclosing sources must be especially careful here. If information relating to a source is held by the data controller then it must be disclosed. If data has been obtained in a commercial setting, it will be extremely unlikely that the data controller will not be holding information on the source.

Example
(This example continues from example 1 earlier in the chapter.) Fiona receives the brochure from Postal Ordering Services Ltd but notices something odd about the address label on the packaging. Her name appears as 'Mrs Fiona E. Pain'. She feels sure that she did not tell the telephone operator her middle name, nor that she was married. She writes a letter to Postal Ordering Services asking for a copy of all the information it holds on her and details of the source of that information. Postal Ordering Services must supply Fiona with the information she has requested and must do so within 40 days of receiving her request plus the £10 maximum fee.

Automated decisions

Section 7(1)(d) provides that where the personal data are being processed automatically for the purpose of evaluating matters relating to the data subject and the processing has or is likely to be the sole basis of a decision significantly affecting the data subject, he or she is entitled to be informed by the data controller of the logic (unless it constitutes a trade secret — s. 8(5)) behind the decision-taking. A common example of such an automated decision-making process is credit scoring. Where a computer program, as a result of information keyed in, decides whether to extend a loan to an individual then the individual concerned is entitled to a description of the decision-making process, i.e., the method by which the decision was reached. There is no requirement in the Act (contrast the right to receive information constituting the personal data and its source) that this information must be communicated in an intelligible form. It is possible that a data controller may be able to comply with the requirement in s. 7(1)(d) by supplying a general statement of the purpose and operation of the relevant software.

See 'Automated decision-taking' below for further discussion on the right to prevent such decisions being made.

Identifying other individuals

In certain cases the data controller will be unable to comply with a request for information without disclosing information relating to another individual who can be identified from the information requested. In determining whether another person can be identified from the information a data controller is entitled to take into account not only the entirety of information that would otherwise be supplied to the data subject but also any information that the data controller reasonably believes is likely to be in the possession (or likely to come into the possession) of the data subject making the request. In the event that another person is likely to be identified the data controller is entitled to refuse to comply with the data subject's request unless (s. 7(4)):

(a)   the other individual has consented to the disclosure of the information to the person making the request, or
(b)   it is reasonable in all the circumstances to comply with the request without the consent of the other individual.

Where the individual who can be identified from the information is in fact the source of the information the data controller is not excused from complying with the request altogether. Here the data controller must disclose so much of the information sought by the data subject as can be communicated without disclosing the identity of the source. This might be done by omitting any references to names or other identifying particulars.

In determining whether it is reasonable in all the circumstances to comply with the request without the consent of the other individual who may be identified, particularly relevant considerations are:

(a)   any duty of confidentiality owed to the individual,
(b)   any steps taken by the data controller with a view to seeking the consent of the individual,
(c)   whether the other individual is capable of giving consent, and
(d)   any express refusal of consent by the individual.

Multiple requests

The data subject is entitled to make as many requests for information from the data controller as he or she sees fit. However, the statute does save the data controller from excess paperwork by providing that a reasonable time must be allowed to elapse between requests. The data controller does not have to comply with a request that has been made too soon after compliance with a previous request. In determining what is a reasonable time for these purposes regard should be had to the following:

(a)   the nature of the data,
(b)   the purpose for which the data are processed, and
(c)   the frequency with which the data are altered.

Amendments to data

It may be, in the course of business or otherwise, that the data will be amended (whether, for example, by addition or deletion) between the time of the data subject's request being received by the data controller and the time of compliance. The information forwarded to the data subject may be the post-amendment version of the data, but only where the 'amendment or deletion would have been made regardless of the receipt of the request' (s. 8(6)).

Credit reference agencies

There are slight modifications to the rights of access provisions in s. 7 where the data controller is a credit reference agency. Section 9 provides that any request for access by a data subject to a credit reference agency will be presumed to be a request for personal data relevant only to the data subject's financial standing. A data subject may rebut that presumption by expressly asking for additional information.

A 'credit reference agency' is 'a person carrying on a business comprising the furnishing of persons with information relevant to the financial standing of individuals, being information collected by the agency for that purpose' (Consumer Credit Act 1974, s. 145(8)).

Where a credit reference agency receives a request for information under the Data Protection Act 1998, s. 7, the obligations of disclosure include a statement (in a form to be prescribed by the Secretary of State) of the individual's rights:

(a)   under the Consumer Credit Act 1974, s. 159 (removal or amendment provisions relating to incorrect information held by an agency (known colloquially as a 'notice of correction') — see appendix 1), and

(b)   to the extent required by the prescribed form.

For specific transitional provisions concerning manual data held by a credit reference agency, see Chapter 5, part 2.

Court order

The right of access to data by data subjects may be enforced by the High Court or a county court (in Scotland by the Court of Session or the sheriff). Where a person has made a request for information (or logic behind decision-taking) and has not been supplied with that information, the court may grant an order requiring the data controller to comply with that request (s. 7(9)). In deciding whether the data subject is entitled to see the information (including the question whether such information is exempt from the provisions — see chapter 5), the court may require access to the information on the basis that it is not shown (at that stage) to the data subject. Assistance from the Commissioner for either party to an application under s. 7(9) is available at the discretion of the Commissioner where a case involves matters of substantial public importance (s. 53).

Transitional exemption

During the first transitional period automated data which is subject to processing which was already underway immediately before 24 October 1998 are exempt from the requirements that the data subject be given:

(a)   a description of the data,
(b)   its purpose and likely receipients,

(c)   the source of the data,
(d)   the logic involved in automated decision-taking.

Eligible manual data are exempt from the subject access provisions in s. 7 during the first transitional period.

For further discussion see Chapter 5, part 2.

PREVENTING PROCESSING: GENERAL

Section 10 provides that where the processing of personal data is causing or is likely to cause *unwarranted and substantial damage* or *unwarranted and substantial distress* to the data subject or another, the data subject is entitled to require the data controller (upon the expiry of a reasonable period) to cease, or not to begin, processing, unless one of the following apply:

(a)   the data subject has given his or her consent to the processing;
(b)   the processing is necessary—
    (i)   for the performance of a contract to which the data subject is a party, or
    (ii)   for the taking of steps at the request of the data subject with a view to entering into a contract;
(c)   the processing is necessary for compliance with any legal obligation to which the data controller is subject, other than an obligation imposed by contract;
(d)   the processing is necessary in order to protect the vital interests of the data subject;
(e)   any other circumstance prescribed by the Secretary of State by order.

In order to take advantage of this power to prevent processing, the data subject must forward to the data controller a notice in writing (a 'data subject notice') and specify the reasons why the processing is or will cause damage or distress. The notice may specify the purpose or manner of processing that is objectionable. The data controller has 21 days from receipt of the notice to make a response. The response (which must be in writing) must consist of one of the following two options:

(a)   a statement that the data controller has complied, or intends to comply, with the request in the data subject notice, or
(b)   a statement that the data controller regards part or all of the data subject notice as unjustified and the extent to which the data controller has complied or intends to comply with it.

Court order

Where a data subject feels that the data controller has failed to comply (in full or in part) with the request in the data subject notice, he or she may apply to the court for an order for compliance. The court will make such an order where it is satisfied that the data subject notice was justified and that the data controller has failed to take such steps to comply with the notice as the court thinks fit (s. 10(4)). Assistance from the Commissioner for either party to an application under s. 10(4) is available at the discretion of the Commissioner where a case involves matters of substantial public importance (s. 53).

Transitional exemption

Eligible automated data and eligible manual data are exempt from the rights in s. 10 during the first transitional period. For further discussion see Chapter 5, part 2.

PREVENTING PROCESSING: DIRECT MARKETING

The marketing strategy known as 'direct marketing' (defined as communication, by whatever means, of any advertising or marketing material which is directed to particular individuals — s. 11(3)) is subject to a right by the data subject to prevent processing for this purpose. An individual may require, under s. 11(1), that the data controller (within a reasonable time) cease, or not begin, processing, for the purposes of direct marketing, personal data of which he or she is the data subject. The request should be in writing. There is no provision which allows the data controller to specify the reasons that the data controller feels the data subject notice to be unjustified. There is no requirement of unwarranted damage or unwarranted distress. There are no exceptions to the right to prevent processing for the purposes of direct marketing. It is interesting to note that a provision in the Bill obliging the data controller to respond to the data subject's request within 21 days has been omitted from the Act. The paperwork that such a provision would have generated would have been prohibitive for data controllers, but the lack of such a provision deprives the data subject of any guaranteed feedback on his or her request for cessation.

The court can order compliance with the data subject notice where it is satisfied that the data controller has failed to comply with the notice. It has power to set out how the data controller should go about doing so.

Example
Janet is sent a letter through the post from Elham International plc inviting her to purchase a product or service. Janet sends a letter to the company requesting it to delete her name, address and any other details from its database. Within a reasonable time of receiving the letter the company must cease processing Janet's personal data for the purposes of direct marketing. Elham International plc may continue to hold the information for other purposes.

Following an appropriate request from a data subject, data held for purposes other than direct marketing should be flagged in some way so that it is not used for direct marketing.

Transitional exemption

During the first transitional period automated data which is subject to processing which was already under way immediately before 24 October 1998 are exempt from the right to prevent processing for direct marketing.

Eligible manual data are exempt from the right to prevent processing during the first transitional period.

For further discussion see Chapter 5, part 2.

AUTOMATED DECISION-TAKING

A data subject has the right to prevent the data controller from taking evaluation decisions concerning him or her by *automated means alone*. Should the individual wish to exercise this right he or she must send a notice in writing requiring the data controller to ensure that no decision taken by or on behalf of the data controller *which significantly affects that individual* is based solely on the processing of personal data by automatic means. Certain decisions are exempt (see below). One class of persons that the statute anticipates may be interested in this right is employees — s. 12(1) gives examples of matters which may be the subject of evaluation by automated processing:

(a)   performance at work,
(b)   creditworthiness,
(c)   reliability,
(d)   conduct.

If an individual has not given proper notice (or even, on one possible construction of s. 12(2), where no notice has been given), and a decision (except an exempt decision) significantly affecting that individual is taken wholly by automated means, the data controller must, as soon as reasonably practicable, inform the individual that such a decision has been taken. The individual then has the right to request the data controller to reconsider the decision or take a new decision on an alternative basis. This right must be exercised within 21 days of receipt by the data subject of the data controller's notification of the decision, and must be exercised in writing (a data subject notice). Due to the ambiguity in the section it is not clear whether this right of the data subject applies universally or whether it applies only where the data subject has sent a notice that no decision should be taken by automated means. It would seem sensible to assume that it is the former, though this will doubtless result in an increase in paperwork for data controllers.

Within 21 days of receipt of the data subject notice, the data controller must inform (in writing) the data subject of the steps the data controller intends to take to comply with the notice.

Court order

A court may order the decision-taker (described in s. 12(8) as 'the responsible person') to reconsider the decision or take a new decision where the data subject can prove that the responsible person has failed:

(a)   to comply with the request from the data subject to ensure that no decision taken which significantly affects him or her is taken solely by automated means, or
(b)   (in the case of the data controller informing the individual of the decision and the data subject requesting reconsideration) to reconsider the, or take a new, decision (s. 12(8)).

Assistance from the Commissioner for either party to an application under s. 7(9) is available at the discretion of the Commissioner where the case involves matters of substantial public importance (s. 53).

Exempt decisions

The requirement that the data subject must be informed of automated decision-taking and have such decisions retaken and the right of the data subject to prevent such decision-taking do not apply to 'exempt decisions'. An exempt decision is one where one of the conditions from each of the following two lists is present. The first list (s. 12(6)) is as follows:

(a)   the decision is taken in the course of steps taken for the purpose of considering whether to enter into a contract with the data subject, or
(b)   the decision is taken in the course of steps taken with a view to entering into such a contract, or
(c)   the decision is taken in the course of steps taken in the course of performing such a contract, or
(d)   the decision is authorised or required by or under any enactment.

The second list (s. 12(7)) contains two alternatives:

(a)   the effect of the decision is to grant a request of the data subject, or
(b)   steps have been taken to safeguard the legitimate interests of the data subject (for example, by allowing him or her to make appropriate comments).

One possible way for a data controller to comply with these requirements is to insert a clear statement in its documentation to the effect that the automated processing system is used to help it consider whether to enter into a contract with the data subject. Then, provided the data subject has asked for such a decision to be taken and either the decision is favourable or there is a right of appeal against an unfavourable decision, the processing will be exempt from the above provisions.

Example
A bank is considering an application by Michael for a loan. It has forwarded standard documentation to Michael which informs him that the decision whether to make the loan will be taken automatically by a computer. Michael reads the documentation and then applies for the loan. The loan was then extended by the bank. The processing of Michael's data is exempt from the right to prevent such processing.

The Secretary of State is empowered to create further exempt decisions by order.

Transitional exemption

During the first transitional period automated data which is subject to processing which was already under way immediately before 24 October 1998 are exempt from the right to request that a decision affecting the data subject is not taken solely by automated means. For further discussion see Chapter 5, part 2.

RECTIFICATION, BLOCKING, ERASURE AND DESTRUCTION

Under s. 14, where a court is satisfied that personal data processed by the data controller are inaccurate (i.e., 'incorrect or misleading as to any matter of fact' — s. 70(2)), it may make an order for the rectification, blocking, erasure or destruction of such data. In addition the court may order the rectification, blocking, erasure or destruction of any personal data which contain an expression of opinion which is based on the inaccurate data. Such rights do not differ markedly from those in the 1984 Act, save that that Act did not mention 'blocking'. There is no definition of this term in the Act and the Commissioner has yet to give an opinion on what it means. It is likely, however, to have its common meaning.

Where the data, despite being inaccurate, accurately reflect information that was passed by the data subject (or a third party) to the data controller, the provisions are somewhat watered down. Here, as an alternative to making an order for rectification, blocking, erasure or destruction, the court may take one of two further courses of action open to it. The first is to make an order requiring the data to be supplemented by a court-approved statement of the true facts relating to the matters dealt with by the data. However, that option is only open to the court where:

(a)   having regard to the purpose or purposes for which the data were obtained and further processed, the data controller has taken reasonable steps to ensure the accuracy of the data, and

(b)   if the data subject has notified the data controller of the data subject's view that the data are inaccurate, the data indicate that fact.

The second (which is only available if either or both of the above two requirements have not been complied with) is to make an order which would have the effect of ensuring compliance with the requirements in (a) and (b) above. This second option may be accompanied by a further order requiring the data to be supplemented by a court-approved statement of the true facts relating to the matters dealt with by the data.

In many cases the inaccurate data held by the data controller will have been passed on to a third party (defined in s. 70(1) as 'any person other than (a) the data subject, (b) the data controller, or (c) any data processor or other person authorised to process data for the data controller or processor'). Where the court orders rectification, blocking, erasure or destruction, or is satisfied by the data subject's claim that personal data which have been rectified, blocked, erased or destroyed were inaccurate, it can, where it is reasonably practicable to do so, make an order that the data controller informs the third party of the rectification, blocking, erasure or destruction. In determining whether it is reasonably practicable to make such an order the court will take into account the number of third parties to whom the inaccurate data have been disclosed.

Additionally, an order for rectification, blocking, erasure or destruction may be made by the court where the data subject is entitled to compensation for damage as a result of the failure of a data controller to comply with any provision of the Act in respect of personal data and there is a substantial risk of further such failure (s. 14(4)). Where the court makes such an order it may order the data controller (unless it is not reasonably practicable to do so) to notify third parties to whom the data have been disclosed of the rectification, blocking, erasure or destruction. In determining whether it is reasonably practicable to make such an order the court will take into account the number of third parties to whom the inaccurate data have been disclosed.

Assistance from the Commissioner for either party to an application under s. 14 is available at the discretion of the Commissioner where a case involves matters of substantial public importance (s. 53).

For further discussion on the transitional right to rectification, blocking, erasure or destruction of 'exempt manual data' see below under 'Transitional rights'.

Transitional exemption

Eligible manual data are exempt from the right to rectification, blocking, erasure and destruction during the first transitional period. Certain eligible manual data are exempt from this right during the second transitional period. For further discussion see Chapter 5, part 2.

COMPENSATION

An individual who suffers damage as a result of a contravention by a data controller of any provision of the Data Protection Act 1998 is entitled to compensation. Compensation for distress may be claimed in all cases where the individual has suffered damage. Compensation for distress without damage may be claimed only where the contravention relates to the processing of data for the 'special purposes', i.e., for the purposes of journalism or for artistic or literary purposes (for further detail on the special purposes see chapter 5, part 1).

Where proceedings are brought against a data controller for compensation it is a defence for the data controller to show that such care was taken as in all the circumstances was reasonably required to comply with the provision concerned.

Assistance from the Commissioner for either party to an application under s. 13 is available at the discretion of the Commissioner where a case involves matters of substantial public importance (s. 53).

Transitional exemption

During the first transitional period automated data which is subject to processing which was already under way immediately before 24 October 1998 are exempt from the right to compensation in s. 13 except where such compensation relates to:

(a) a contravention of the fourth data protection principle,
(b) a disclosure without the consent of the data controller,
(c) loss or destruction of data without the consent of the data controller, or
(d) processing for the special purposes.

Eligible manual data are exempt from the right to compensation during the first transitional period. For further discussion see Chapter 5, part 2.

TRANSITIONAL RIGHTS

Further rights of data subjects in respect of exempt manual data are conveyed until 23 October 2007 by sch. 13 which adds a s. 12A to the Act until that time. 'Exempt manual data' for these purposes means:

(a)   from the commencement of the schedule to 23 October 2001, eligible manual data forming part of an accessible record (whether or not processing was already under way on 24 October 1998), and

(b)   from 24 October 2001 to 23 October 2007, eligible manual data (other than data which are processed only for the purpose of historical research) which were held immediately before 24 October 1998 and any other personal data forming part of an accessible record.

For the definition of 'eligible manual data' see chapter 5, part 2.

Under s. 12A(1) a data subject is entitled at any time by notice in writing to require the data controller:

(a)   to rectify, block, erase or destroy exempt manual data which are inaccurate or incomplete, or

(b)   to cease holding exempt manual data in a way incompatible with the legitimate purposes pursued by the data controller.

The notice must state the data subject's reasons for believing either of these matters (s. 12A(2)). If the data controller fails to comply with such a notice then the data subject may apply to the court for an order for compliance (s. 12A(3)). The court will grant such an order against the data controller where it feels that the notice was justified and that the data controller has failed to comply.

Assistance from the Commissioner for either party to an application under s. 12A is available at the discretion of the Commissioner where a case involves matters of substantial public importance (s. 53).

Chapter 3
Data Protection Principles

INTRODUCTION

The data protection principles are listed in sch. 1 to the Data Protection Act 1998. The principles form the backbone of the legislation and their importance is underlined by the extent of the powers of the Data Protection Commissioner in relation to the issuing of information and enforcement notices (see chapter 6).

To those who are familiar with the data protection principles in the 1984 Act, the new principles may, at first sight, appear similar. However this apparent familiarity can be misleading. As Graham Sutton (head of the Data Protection Bill drafting team at the Home Office) has pointed out, the old principles are 'false friends'. This is due to the fact that although they may appear substantially similar to the new principles, the very wide meaning of processing and the lack of registered purposes under the new provisions means that their effect is radically different. There are still eight in number, but the text of the first seven contains slightly more detail than before. The eighth principle in the new Act did not appear in the 1984 Act. It relates to the prohibition on transferring personal data to countries that do not have an adequate level of protection for the rights and freedoms of data subjects.

This chapter will set out each of the eight principles and go on to discuss their application. Decisions of the Data Protection Tribunal and the courts are cited where they are a relevant extra-statutory aid to the interpretation of the principles. Schedule 1 is divided into two parts — part I lists the eight principles and part II gives helpful guidance on the interpretation of the principles.

FIRST PRINCIPLE

Personal data shall be processed fairly and lawfully and, in particular, shall not be processed unless—

    (a)   at least one of the conditions in Schedule 2 is met, and

    (b)   in the case of sensitive personal data, at least one of the conditions in Schedule 3 is also met.

The first principle is more extensive than its counterpart in the 1984 Act. This is due to the fact that the definition of processing is considerably wider under the new provisions — see chapter 2.

Processing will not be lawful unless one of the conditions in Schedule 2 is met. In the case of sensitive personal data, processing will not be lawful unless one of the conditions in Schedule 2 and one of the conditions in Schedule 3 are met.

Compliance with Schedule 2, and where relevant Schedule 3, does not guarantee that the processing will be fair and lawful. It may well be that the processing in question is unfair or unlawful (and thus not in compliance with the first principle) for another reason (see for example, the *British Gas* case below). Furthermore, the processing may breach another of the principles or a provision in another statute.

The following discussion of the first principle will assume that none of the exemptions apply. For a discussion of the exemptions see Chapter 5.

Obtaining data

The 1984 Act required data to be both 'obtained' and 'processed' fairly. The new provision relates only to processing, but the definition of processing (see chapter 2) now includes 'obtaining'. Case law relating to the definition of 'obtaining' personal data therefore remains relevant. It is essential that data controllers obtain information correctly, i.e., in accordance with the first principle. Failure to do so puts all subsequent processing in jeopardy. Not only must data be obtained fairly within the guidelines in Schedule 1, part II, but the obtaining itself must meet the relevant Schedule 2 and Schedule 3 conditions (see below).

The interpretation provisions in Schedule 1 state that regard must be had to the method of obtaining the data in determining whether the processing is fair. It is clear that processing will be unfair where any person from whom it has been obtained is deceived or misled as to its intended purpose.

In *Innovations (Mail Order) Ltd* v *Data Protection Registrar* (DA92 31/49/1) a mail order company obtained business in two principal ways: by receiving orders from its catalogues and by receiving orders in response to its advertisements in the media. Customers were informed of the possibility of their details being used for other purposes only after their details had been obtained. The company engaged in the practice known as 'list rental' (trading in lists of customers names and addresses) and names of customers from both categories were used for this purpose. It was the Registrar's contention that all customers had to be informed of all intended uses for their personal details at the time the order was made. The company argued that the practical constraints this would cause for their general media advertising made this impractical. The Data Protection Tribunal found that the absence of a warning in the general media advertising might lead to an assumption on the part of individual members of the public that their details would not be traded. This meant that some members of the public would be misled and therefore that the obtaining of the information was unfair.

Information to be supplied to the data subject

According to sch. 1, part II, para. 2(1)(a) and (3), data obtained from the data subject will not be treated as processed fairly, and hence will breach the first principle, unless the data controller ensures (so far as is practicable) that the data subject has, or has ready access to, the following information:

(a)   the identity of the data controller,
(b)   the identity of any representative of the data controller,

(c)   the purpose or purposes for which the data are intended to be processed, and
(d)   any other information which is necessary to enable processing to be fair.

The giving of such information to the data subject was dealt with in Article 10 of the Directive and is commonly referred to as 'Article 10 Notice'.

It is interesting to note that as far as paragraph (d) is concerned, the information needed to be transmitted to the data subject to enable the processing to be fair could extend to informing her of the right to object to direct marketing (see Chapter 2).

According to para. 2(1)(b) and (3) where data have *not* been obtained from the data subject, processing will be unfair unless the data controller ensures (so far as is practicable) that, 'before the relevant time or as soon as practicable after that time', the data subject has or has ready access to the information in (a) to (d) above ('Article 11 Notice'). For these purposes, by para. 2(2) 'the relevant time' means:

(a)   the time when the data controller first processes the data, or
(b)   in a case where, at the time of first processing, there is likely to be disclosure of the data to a third person within a reasonable period:
    (i)   where the data are so disclosed, the time when that occurs,
    (ii)   the time when the data controller becomes, or ought to become, aware that the data are unlikely to be disclosed within that reasonable period, or
    (iii)   the end of that reasonable period.

There is no definition of 'reasonable period' in the Act. The Data Protection Commissioner is expected to issue advice about what may constitute a reasonable period, which may vary according to circumstances. It is likely to depend on the type of processing in question, the effect on the data subject and the ease of providing such information.

Example
A market researcher telephones Susie and asks her for information about her shopping habits. Susie tells the researcher which supermarket she uses and gives a list of some basic products that she and her husband, Mark, commonly purchase. Mark must be informed, as soon as practicable after the telephone conversation takes place, of the identity of the researcher or the researcher's employer and the purpose of requiring the information that Susie has given. Where the market researcher is acting as agent for another, Mark must be informed of those matters within a reasonable period.

Where the data controller did not obtain the information from the data subject there is an exception to the obligation to notify the data subject of the matters listed in (a) to (d) above. This applies where one of the following two primary conditions (set out in para. 3(2)) is true:

(a)   the provision of that information would involve a disproportionate effort, or
(b)   the recording of the information to be contained in the data by, or the disclosure of the data by, the data controller is necessary for compliance with any legal obligation to which the data controller is subject, other than an obligation imposed by contract.

Where information is obtained from a third party and one of the above primary conditions applies, the obligation to inform the data subject is nullified. There is no definition of 'disproportionate' in the Act. It would seem to relate to the consequences of the activity for the data subject. Where the effort needed to contact the data subject is considerable, this is likely to constitute disproportionate effort unless it is outweighed by the consequences for the data subject, e.g., because it involves significant, or otherwise important, processing. The second of the two primary conditions would apply where the data controller is under a statutory duty to obtain details about the data subject from a third party.

Example
Katie's grandmother is soon to be 80. For her birthday Katie arranges for a bouquet of flowers to be sent to her by the local florist. If the florist records the name and address of grandmother, the provisions of the first principle require the florist to give Katie's grandmother the relevant information, thus ruining the surprise. The telephone conversation to the grandmother might be along the following lines: 'We have information about you concerning the delivery of flowers. Please try to act surprised when they arrive. (This scenario was foreseen by the Home Office and much discussed at the Committee stage of the Bill.)

It could be argued, in relation to the above example that it is 'not practicable' to supply the grandmother with the relevant information because the surprise will be ruined. Such an argument seems tenuous and the sophistry involved could perhaps be circumvented by arguing that the grandmother need not be contacted because the effort involved would be 'disproportionate' to any gain made by the grandmother. It is unknown whether employment of the first primary conditon in this manner would remedy the problem. There is no definition of 'disproportionate effort' in the Act nor in the Directive. It could be argued that the first primary condition will only apply where the data controller has obtained a massive database of personal data so as to obviate the need to contact every data subject immediately.

Paragraph 3(1) empowers the Secretary of State to prescribe further conditions to determine what would constitute an exemption from the need to inform the data subject where information is obtained from a third party. However, the wording of the provision is ambiguous and could be construed to mean that the primary conditions will not operate without such prescribed condition or conditions (if any are made) *also* being present, i.e., in addition to the primary conditions. This turns on the construction of 'together with' in para. 3(1). One possible construction is that any prescribed conditions will be additional to, and separate from, the primary conditions. The alternative construction is that any additional conditions so prescribed will be unable to operate on their own, but will require the presence of one of the primary conditions. At the time of writing no further conditions have been prescribed.

Presumption of fairness

There is a presumption in para. 1(2) that data will have been obtained fairly where obtained from a person who:

(a)   is authorised by or under any enactment to supply it, or
(b)   is required to supply it by or under any enactment or by any convention or other instrument imposing an international obligation on the UK.

However, the presumption will only apply where the data subject has been supplied with the information required by para. 2 (see above).

Tribunal precedent

There is a dearth of actual precedent on what may and may not amount to fair processing. However one example arose in the case of *British Gas* v *Data Protection Registrar* (1998) which was an appeal against an enforcement notice which has been issued in July 1997 under the old legislation. The enforcement notice claimed that British Gas was contravening the first data protection principle by unfairly and unlawfully processing personal data relating to individual customers for the supply of gas.

As far as lawfulness was concerned the Registrar claimed that British Gas had acted *ultra vires*, in breach of:

(a)   s. 42 of the Gas Act 1986,
(b)   an implied contractual term, and
(c)   confidence.

The Data Protection Tribunal dismissed all of these claims. However, the Registrar was more successful in its claim that British Gas had acted unfairly. Essentially the relevant facts were that British Gas had two main databases, a tariff gas bill database and a marketing database. In early 1997 the company enclosed a leaflet entitled 'Your Data Protection Rights' with each gas bill that it sent out. The leaflet stated that British Gas wished to:

(a)   write to its customers about its products and services,
(b)   send to its customers information about products and services offered by other reputable organisations, and
(c)   pass on information about customers to other companies in the British Gas Group so that customers could receive information about those companies' products and services directly from them.

If customers did not wish to receive such information they could decline by returning a form to British Gas. The registrar felt this to be unfair — in the case of a monopoly utility. Customers should be required to opt in rather than opt out.

In determining the issue of fairness the Tribunal took into account the monopoly (as it then was) of British Gas and found the processing of personal data for disclosure to third parties for marketing purposes was unfair unless done with the consent of the data user. (It is interesting to note that under the new legislation the first principle would be breached (by virtue of Schedule 2) on the same set of facts where a customer did not give consent.)

Criteria for lawful processing

For processing to be lawful at least one of the conditions in sch. 2 must be met. There are no exceptions to this rule. The first condition relates to the data subject giving his or her consent to the processing, and is likely to be the most important. In many cases, such as list rental, the first condition is the only one that could possibly apply.

The six conditions set out in sch. 2 are as follows:

1.   The data subject has given his consent to the processing.

There is no definition of consent in the Act. At the time of drafting the Bill, it was the view of the Home Office that the courts know what consent means, thus rendering a definition unnecessary. Article 7(a) of the European Directive speaks of 'unambiguous' consent. Again the Home Office felt this distinction unnecessary when drafting the Bill and preferred the view that ambiguous consent is not consent. It will of course be for the data controller to decide, in the first instance, what is meant by consent. The data controller's view will be subject to that of the Commissioner and ultimately the courts.

What amounts to consent may depend on the identity of the person consenting as well as on the form that such consent takes. In the *British Gas* case (above) the Data Protection Tribunal drew a distinction between new and existing customers for the purpose of determining when the requirement of consent would be satisfied. New customers could indicate their acquiescence at the time of entering into the agreement for the supply of gas or in a document returned by the customer to confirm the arrangements for the supply of gas (such as either an opt-in box ticked or an opt-out box left blank). With existing customers it would not be enough simply to send them a leaflet giving them an opportunity to object to the processing of information beyond gas-related purposes. Consent would however be made out, said the Tribunal, where such customers were informed of the likely use for the data and were given a choice to agree or not and either consented then and there or did not object to such use. Alternatively, a form could be used which indicated consent or, by not filling in an opt-out box, indicated no objection to the proposed processing. The Tribunal made it clear that there must be some response to British Gas, i.e., that a failure to respond cannot be taken as consent. The case was of course under the old legislation.

2.   The processing is necessary—
     (a)   for the performance of a contract to which the data subject is a party, or
     (b)   for the taking of steps at the request of the data subject with a view to entering into a contract.

Data controllers' contracts with data subjects should contain data protection clauses which deal expressly with this issue.

3.   The processing is necessary for compliance with any legal obligation to which the data controller is subject, other than an obligation imposed by contract.

Any statutory or other legal obligation imposed on the data controller will ensure compliance with Schedule 2 where the processing is necessary to comply with that obligation. Contractual obligations, covered by condition 2, are excluded from condition 3.

4.   The processing is necessary in order to protect the vital interests of the data subject.

The word 'vital' is key to this condition and is likely to be construed narrowly. The European Directive speaks of protecting an interest which is 'essential for the data subject's life'. An emergency situation would therefore be covered. So too would be something of very great importance to the data subject.

5.   The processing is necessary—
   (a)   for the administration of justice,
   (b)   for the exercise of any functions conferred on any person by or under any enactment,
   (c)   for the exercise of any functions of the Crown, a Minister of the Crown or a government department, or
   (d)   for the exercise of any other functions of a public nature exercised in the public interest by any person.

This condition will cover many public-sector data controllers. The last of the four alternatives is drafted somewhat more widely than the first three and there is no definition of public interest. This condition might extend to the processing of closed-circuit television images.

6.—(1)   The processing is necessary for the purposes of legitimate interests pursued by the data controller or by the third party or parties to whom the data are disclosed, except where the processing is unwarranted in any particular case by reason of prejudice to the rights and freedoms or legitimate interests of the data subject.

The starting point here is the existence of legitimate interests of the data controller. The processing must be necessary for those legitimate interests and must not be unwarranted. The processing will be unwarranted where it is prejudicial to the rights, freedoms or legitimate interests of the data subject. Thus a balancing of the interests of the data controller as against the data subject is key to this condition. Where the processing is detrimental to the interests of the data subject then those interests are likely to override the interests of the data controller.

The Secretary of State may by order specify circumstances in which this condition will or will not be satisfied. Such a widely drawn power could, in theory, legitimise any processing by a data controller by deeming it to outweigh the interests of the data subject.

Sensitive personal data

The Data Protection Act 1998 effectively creates a new category of sensitive personal data (defined below). The 1984 Act gave the Secretary of State the power to make regulations in relation to 'sensitive data', but no such regulations were ever made.

A data controller who processes sensitive personal data must, in addition to satisfying one of the criteria in Schedule 2, also comply with one of the conditions in Schedule 3. It is thus vital for data controllers to check all sensitive processing to see that it complies with one of the provisions. The term 'sensitive personal data' is defined in s. 2 as meaning:

personal data consisting of information as to—

    (a)   the racial or ethnic origin of the data subject,

    (b)   his political opinions,

    (c)   his religious beliefs or other beliefs of a similar nature,

    (d)   whether he is a member of a trade union,

    (e)   his physical or mental health or condition,

    (f)   his sexual life,

    (g)   the commission or alleged commission by him of any offence, or

    (h)   any proceedings for any offence committed or alleged to have been committed by him, the disposal of such proceedings or the sentence of any court in such proceedings.

There is likely to be considerable argument over precisely what is meant by each of these descriptions of types of information. Some will cause greater argument than others. Could the racial or ethnic origin of a data subject, for example, be gleaned from his or her surname or family name (e.g., Jones, Patel, McGregor, Abdullah)? If so, this would seem to result in a data subject's name being sensitive personal data.

The conditions for the lawful processing of sensitive personal data are set out in sch. 3 and may be summarised as follows:

1.   The data subject has given his explicit consent to the processing of the personal data.

This condition is likely to be the most commonly used. The distinction between 'explicit consent' in Schedule 3 and 'consent' in Schedule 2 is unclear, but it is likely that explicit consent will not be made out where the data subject is not fully informed of all the relevant facts in relation to the proposed processing. This condition will no doubt require a rewording of the pre-1998 Act data protection notices. Instead of a box being provided for a data subject to opt out of further processing, a box could be provided requiring a data subject to fill in a tick if he or she consents to processing (an opt-in clause). Alternatively, notice could be worded in such a way that it amounted to consent.

Explicit consent given as required by sch. 3, para. 1, would also operate to legitimise the processing for Schedule 2 purposes. In order to be sure of compliance with this first condition, data controllers should ensure that they are in possession of proof of explicit consent.

2.   The processing is necessary for the purposes of exercising or performing any right or obligation which is conferred or imposed by law on the data controller in connection with employment.

Sensitive personal data may be processed to comply with employment law obligations. The Secretary of State may produce regulations which exclude the operation of this condition or specify further conditions that are to be complied with in certain circumstances (para. 2(2)).

3.   The processing is necessary to protect the vital interests of the data subject or another person.

This condition can only be invoked where:

(a)   consent cannot be given by, or on behalf of, the data subject, or
(b)   the data controller cannot reasonably be expected to obtain the consent of the data subject, or
(c)   (in a case concerning the protection of the vital interests of another person) consent by or on behalf of the data subject has been unreasonably withheld.

Vital interests, as in Schedule 2, para. 4, are life-threatening circumstances. Health data are likely to benefit from this condition, such as where a data subject has a communicable disease and 'another person' is in danger of infection. The data subject could not give consent if he or she is unconscious or cannot be found. If the data subject simply refuses permission, a data controller which is a health authority would be able to utilise the third alternative above. Emergency situations should be covered by this condition.

4.   The processing is carried out as part of the legitimate activities of a not-for-profit body or association.

In order to take advantage of this condition the body or association must exist for political, philosophical, religious or trade-union purposes and the processing must:

(a)   be carried out with appropriate safeguards for the rights and freedoms of data subjects,
(b)   relate only to individuals who either are members of the body or association or have regular contact with it in connection with its purposes, and
(c)   not involve disclosure of the personal data to a third party without the consent of the data subject.

5.   The information contained in the personal data has been made public as a result of steps deliberately taken by the data subject.

Where the data subject has introduced sensitive personal data into the public domain it will not be a breach of the first data protection principle to process such information.

6.   The processing is necessary in relation to legal rights.

Here the processing must be necessary for one of the following three purposes:

(a)   obtaining legal advice,
(b)   establishing, exercising or defending legal rights, or
(c)   the conduct of any legal proceedings (including prospective legal proceedings).

7.   The processing is necessary—
     (a)   for the administration of justice,
     (b)   for the exercise of any functions conferred on any person by or under an enactment, or

(c)   for the exercise of any functions of the Crown, a Minister of the Crown or a government department.

This condition does not appear in the European Directive. However, Member States are permitted to make additional conditions where they incorporate 'suitable safeguards' and are in the public interest. No such safeguards appear in the Schedule.

The Secretary of State may exclude the operation of, or attach additional requirements to, this condition as he sees fit (para. 7(2)).

8.   The processing is necessary for medical purposes.

For this condition to apply the processing must be undertaken by a health professional or someone who owes a similar duty of confidentiality. Medical purposes is defined fairly widely to include:

(a)   preventative medicine,
(b)   medical diagnosis,
(c)   medical research
(d)   the provision of care and treatment,
(e)   management of healthcare services.

This is not an exhaustive list and therefore other medical purposes could fall within the definition. The Directive's definition of medical purposes did not include 'medical research'. This has been a controversial addition to the Act by the UK government.

9.   The processing is necessary to trace equality of opportunity between peoples of different racial or ethnic backgrounds.

This condition was added by the Commons at the committee stage and relates to the need to do research on, and keep records in relation to, equality of opportunity. It relates only to the first category of sensitive data, i.e., information relating to racial or ethnic origin. The processing must be with a view to the promotion or maintenance of equality of opportunity and there must be appropriate safeguards for the rights and freedoms of data subjects.

The Secretary of State may specify circumstances in which it will be deemed that processing has, or has not, been carried out with appropriate safeguards.

10.   Any other condition made by the Secretary of State.

The Secretary of State is empowered to list specific circumstances which will legitimise the processing of sensitive personal data. The Directive requires such additional circumstances to be in the public interest and to contain suitable safeguards. These requirements are missing from the Act.

General identifiers

Schedule 1, part II, para. 4, envisages secondary legislation in respect of 'general identifiers' by providing that personal data which contain a general identifier (falling within a description prescribed by the Secretary of State) will not comply with the first principle unless there is compliance with any relevant provision laid down by the Secretary of State (at the time of writing there have been no such provisions). A 'general identifier' is:

> any identifier (such as, for example, a number or code used for identification purposes) which—
>
> (a)   relates to an individual, and
> (b)   forms part of a set of similar identifiers which is of general application.

Examples of general identifiers are National Health Service numbers and National Insurance numbers.

If no regulations are made by the Secretary of State then there will be no restriction, as far as the first principle is concerned, on the processing of a general identifier. However, it may be that the processing of a general identifier breaches another of the principles.

AM I PROCESSING DATA FAIRLY?

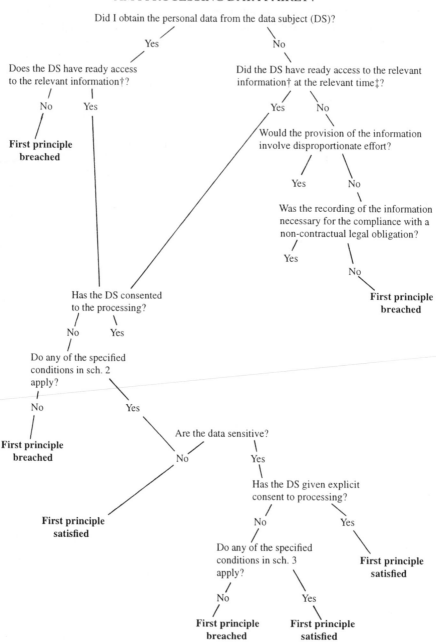

Did I obtain the personal data from the data subject (DS)?

Yes — Does the DS have ready access to the relevant information†?
- No → **First principle breached**
- Yes → Has the DS consented to the processing?

No — Did the DS have ready access to the relevant information† at the relevant time‡?
- Yes → Has the DS consented to the processing?
- No → Would the provision of the information involve disproportionate effort?
  - Yes → Was the recording of the information necessary for the compliance with a non-contractual legal obligation?
    - Yes
    - No → **First principle breached**
  - No

Has the DS consented to the processing?
- No → Do any of the specified conditions in sch. 2 apply?
  - No → **First principle breached**
  - Yes → Are the data sensitive?
    - No → **First principle satisfied**
    - Yes → Has the DS given explicit consent to processing?
      - No → Do any of the specified conditions in sch. 3 apply?
        - No → **First principle breached**
        - Yes → **First principle satisfied**
      - Yes → **First principle satisfied**
- Yes

†The information specified in sch. 1, part II, para. 2(3)   ‡The time defined in sch. 1, part II, para. 2(2)

SECOND PRINCIPLE

Personal data shall be obtained only for one or more specified and lawful purposes, and shall not be processed in any manner incompatible with that purpose or those purposes.

The first and second principles both concern the obtaining and other processing of information. The interpretation guidance in sch. 1, part II, para. 5, states that the purpose or purposes for which personal data are obtained may be specified:

(a) in a notice given by the data controller to the data subject, or
(b) in a notification given to the Commissioner under part III of the Act.

Data are not to be processed in a manner inconsistent with the purpose for which they were obtained. In determining whether the manner of processing is compatible with that purpose, one of the factors to bear in mind is the purpose or purposes for which the personal data are intended to be processed by any person to whom they are disclosed (sch. 1, part II, para. 6).

In the *British Gas* case (see above) the Registrar claimed that Brtish Gas had contravened the second and third principles in the 1984 Act (which taken together, had substantially similar wording to the second principle in the 1998 Act) by holding, using and disclosing customer details for the purpose of debt collection and tracing. This was not challenged by British Gas who took steps to discontinue the practice.

THIRD PRINCIPLE

Personal data shall be adequate, relevant and not excessive in relation to the purpose or purposes for which they are processed.

There are no interpretation provisions for the third principle in the Act. However, this principle does not differ in any significant way from the equivalent principle (the fourth) in the 1984 Act (save that the 1998 Act applies to certain manual records and purposes are no longer clearly defined registered purposes).

Tribunal litigation on this principle arose out of the community charge (or 'poll tax') regime. Various data subjects complained that information held about them for the purposes of administering the community charge was more than was required for the purpose. The Data Protection Registrar refused the applications to register of several local authorities on this basis. In *Community Charge Registration Officers of Runnymede Borough Council, South Northamptonshire District Council and Harrow Borough Council* v *Data Protection Registrar* (DA/90 24/49/3) the Tribunal found that, whilst the holding of 'some additional information' was permissible in certain circumstances, the holding on a database of a substantial quantity of property information obtained from voluntary answers on the canvass forms was far more than was necessary for the purpose.

In a similar case (*Community Charge Registration Officer of Rhondda Borough Council* v *Data Protection Registrar* (DA/90 25/49/2)) the CCRO for Rhondda continued to request dates of birth from individuals on community charge forms after the Registrar suggested that such information should be excluded from the forms, save in exceptional circumstances. The CCRO contended that the dates of birth were necessary for distinguishing between people in an area in which many had both last and first names in common. Despite a lack of statistics the Tribunal accepted that there could be more persons with names in common in Rhondda than in other parts of the country. However, the appellant did not seek to limit the database to only hold dates of birth of persons who were living at the same address with identical names. The Tribunal held that:

> the information the appellant wishes to hold on database concerning individuals exceeds substantially the minimum amount of information which is required in order for him to fulfil the purposes for which he has sought registration namely to fulfil his duty to compile and maintain the Community Charges Register. . . . We are satisfied by the evidence before us that the wide and general extent of the information about dates of birth is irrelevant and excessive.

In similar circumstances today a data controller could comply with the third principle by inserting an instruction as follows: 'Please provide your date of birth only if there is another person living in your house with both the same last and first name as you'.

FOURTH PRINCIPLE

Personal data shall be accurate and, where necessary, kept up to date.

The fourth principle will not be breached where inaccurate information in personal data accurately records information obtained from the data subject or a third party if the data controller has taken reasonable steps to ensure the accuracy of the data (sch. 1, part II, para. 7). Where the data subject has informed the data controller of the inaccuracy of the data, the data must indicate that fact. Thus the data controller is under an obligation to take reasonable steps to verify the accuracy of the data obtained. What is reasonable will depend on the circumstances and particularly on the purpose for which the data were obtained.

The use of 'markers' as provided for in s. 22 of the 1984 Act is no longer a satisfactory way of complying with this principle.

FIFTH PRINCIPLE

Personal data processed for any purpose or purposes shall not be kept for longer than is necessary for that purpose or those purposes.

As with the third principle there is very little difference between this principle and its counterpart in the 1984 Act and the wording is self-explanatory. Keeping data beyond the length of time necessary for the purpose for which the data were processed will breach the fifth principle. There are no interpretative provisions in the Act.

Purposes are no longer clearly defined registered purposes as they were in the 1984 Act.

SIXTH PRINCIPLE

Personal data shall be processed in accordance with the rights of data subjects under this Act.

Schedule 1, part II, para. 8, states that a person will breach this principle only if he:

(a)   contravenes the rights of access provisions in s. 7,

(b)   fails to comply with a justified request to cease processing under s. 10 or fails to respond to such a request within 21 days of its receipt,

(c)   fails to comply with a request under s. 11 to cease direct marketing processing,

(d)   contravenes s. 13 by failing to comply with a request in relation to automated decision-taking (either to prevent such a decision being taken or to have it reconsidered) or failing to notify the data subject that a decision was taken on such a basis or failing to reply to the data subject within 21 days of the receipt of such a request, or

(e)   contravenes s. 12A (see chapter 2, 'Transitional rights') by failing to comply with a notice given under subsection (1) of that section to the extent that the notice is justified.

SEVENTH PRINCIPLE

Appropriate technical and organisational measures shall be taken against unauthorised or unlawful processing of personal data and against accidental loss or destruction of, or damage to, personal data.

The seventh principle provides, in essence, that appropriate care must be taken of personal data. The interpretation provisions in Schedule 1, part II, paras 9 to 12, suggest that account must be taken of the state of technology (and its cost) available at the relevant time. The protective measures must ensure a level of security which is appropriate to the harm which might result from the events mentioned in the seventh principle and the nature of the data to be protected. Data Controllers should monitor changes in technology so that they do not inadvertantly breach the seventh principle by failing to upgrade existing systems.

There is an obligation on the data controller to ensure the reliability of all employees who have access to personal data. This obligation applies so far as is reasonable in the circumstances. Doubtless the familiar balancing test should be employed, with a greater degree of training being needed where there is a greater importance that the data be secure.

Data processors

A 'data processor' is defined in s. 1(1) as 'any person (other than an employee of the data controller) who processes the data on behalf of the data controller'. Where processing is to be carried out by a data processor the data controller must choose the data processor with care and, in particular, should ensure the provision of sufficient guarantees by the data processor in relation to appropriate security measures (sch. 1, part II, para. 11). Additionally the data controller must take reasonable steps to ensure that the data processor complies with such security measures. The arrangement for processing between the data controller and the data processor must be contractual and evidenced in writing (para. 12). The contract must be exclusive in respect of the data processor's instructions concerning the data, and must oblige the data processor to comply with the obligations contained in the seventh principle.

Where data are processed by one company on behalf of another (even where the companies are part of the same group) there must be a written contract between them — informal arrangements are insufficient — and it must require the processor to comply with the provisions of the seventh principle. The data controller's obligation to check the processor's security measures could be undertaken by the submission of a detailed questionnaire to prospective data processors before an appointment is made.

EIGHTH PRINCIPLE

Personal data shall not be transferred to a country or territory outside the European Economic Area unless that country or territory ensures an adequate level of protection for the rights and freedoms of data subjects in relation to the processing of personal data.

This principle is new to UK data protection legislation and results from the Directive's aim of harmonisation of the European Union's data protection measures. The European Economic Area consists of the 15 Member States of the European Union plus Norway, Iceland and Liechtenstein. There is no restriction on the transfer of information between those countries.

A transfer of personal data to any other country is unlawful unless that country has an adequate level of protection for such data. Schedule 1, part II, para. 13, contains some guidance on what will be regarded as 'adequate'. Regard must be had to:

(a)   the nature of the personal data;
(b)   the country or territory of origin of the information contained in the data;
(c)   the country or territory of final destination of that information;
(d)   the purposes for which and period during which the data are intended to be processed;
(e)   the law in force in the country or territory in question;
(f)   the international obligations of that country or territory;
(g)   any relevant codes of conduct or other rules which are enforceable in that country or territory (whether generally or by arrangement in particular cases);
(h)   any security measures taken in respect of the data in that country or territory.

This list is not exhaustive. There is no mention of the factor which may well be the most relevant of all: the terms of the contract between the transferor and transferee. Article 26 of the European Directive refers to 'appropriate contractual solutions' as an additional factor for consideration. That the contract itself could provide an adequate level of protection is a somewhat controversial position, but one that could find favour with the Commissioner. The eighth principle itself suggests that it is the country of the transferee that must provide the protection. However, it is at least arguable that if the provisions of the contract are enforceable in that country's legal system then that country is in fact providing such protection. Further, where the contract provides for security measures to be taken in respect of the data when they arrive abroad, such a factor is one of the specified matters to be taken into account in determining adequacy. The International Chamber of Commerce and the Confederation of British Industry have drafted a model set of contractual terms in an attempt to meet the requirements of the eighth principle.

Article 25 of the Directive envisages the European Commission making pronouncements on whether any given country does, or does not, ensure an adequate level of protection. Such a finding of the Commission is binding in all proceedings concerning such an issue in each Member State, including the UK (sch. 1, part II, para. 15). Thus a data controller can be sure that the transfer of personal data to such a 'cleared' country does not contravene the eighth principle.

Transitional provisions

Compliance with the eighth principle is not necessary, for processing already under way, until 23 October 2001 (see chapter 5, part 2).

Exemptions

Schedule 4 sets out cases where the eighth principle does not apply. Under it the eighth principle does not prevent trans-border data flows where:

(a)   The data subject has given his consent to the transfer.

(b)   The transfer is necessary for the entering into a contract between the data controller and the data subject or for the performance of such a contract.

(c)   The transfer is necessary for the performance or conclusion of a contract between the data controller and a third party which is:

(i)   entered into at the request of the data subject, or
(ii)   in the interests of the data subject.

(d)   The transfer is necessary for reasons of substantial public interest (the Secretary of State is empowered to specify circumstances which will amount to substantial public interest).

(e)   The transfer is necessary for legal proceedings, for obtaining legal advice or establishing, exercising or defending legal rights.

(f)   The transfer is necessary in order to protect the vital interests of the data subject (as to what this means see above).

(g)   The transfer is to a person who could have obtained the personal data from a public register.

(h)   The transfer is of a kind approved by the Commissioner for the purposes of the eighth principle.

(i)   The transfer has been authorised by the Commissioner.

AM I TRANSFERRING DATA IN CONTRAVENTION OF THE EIGHTH PRINCIPLE?

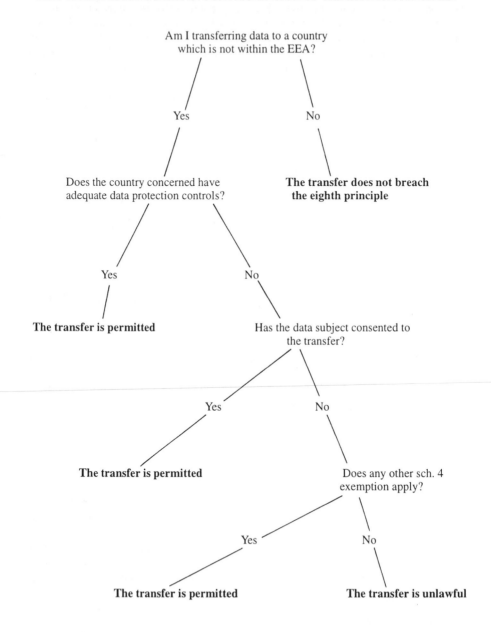

Am I transferring data to a country
which is not within the EEA?

Yes — Does the country concerned have
adequate data protection controls?

No — **The transfer does not breach
the eighth principle**

Yes — **The transfer is permitted**

No — Has the data subject consented to
the transfer?

Yes — **The transfer is permitted**

No — Does any other sch. 4
exemption apply?

Yes — **The transfer is permitted**

No — **The transfer is unlawful**

Chapter 4
Notification by Data Controllers

INTRODUCTION

The notification procedure under the Data Protection Act 1998 is slightly less formal than under the 1984 Act. The new regime requires a data controller to send a list of information to the Commissioner together with a fee. Subject to certain exceptions, the processing of personal data without notification is a criminal offence.

Article 18(1) of the Directive provides that:

> Member States shall provide that the [data] controller or his representative, if any, must notify the supervisory authority ... before carrying out any wholly or partly automatic processing operation or set of such operations intended to serve a single purpose or several related purposes.

Much of the detail on notification remains unknown at the time of writing since the regulations have yet to be made by the Secretary of State. The updated edition of this book, due to be published towards the end of 1999, will contain a full analysis of the notification regulations.

A data controller who has registered its processing with the Data Protection Registrar under the provisions of the old Act need not notify under the new Act until the expiry of its existing registration (for further details see chapter eight under 'Effect of 1984 Act registration').

PROHIBITION ON PROCESSING

Section 17(1) provides that the processing of personal data will be unlawful (and under s. 21(1) a criminal offence) where all of the following apply:

(a)   an entry in the register maintained by the Commissioner has not been made,

(b)   the notification regulations (if any) relating to deemed registration do not apply,

(c)   notification regulations (if any) giving authority to certain specified types of processing without the need for notification do not apply, and

(d)   it is not the case that the sole purpose of the processing is the maintenance of a public register.

Therefore, generally speaking the processing of personal data will be unlawful where it has not been notified to the commissioner.

However, the prohibition in s. 17 applies only to personal data which consist of information which falls within the first two paragraphs of the definition of 'data' (i.e., being or intended to be automatically processed). Processing of personal data without registration is therefore lawful (unless it is 'assessable processing' — see below) where it consists of information which:

(a)   is recorded as part of a relevant filing system, or
(b)   forms part of an accessible record (see definition in chapter 2).

Therefore the processing of manual records (or accessible records), even if they fall within the definition of data in the new Act, is not subject to notification to the Commissioner. Voluntary notification under s. 18 is possible for processors of manual data. Where voluntary notification does not take place, the data controller is subject to the disclosure provisions in s. 24 — see 'Duty of disclosure' below.

A data controller who both manually and automatically processes personal data will need to notify in respect of the automatically processed data and may do so in respect of the manual (or accessible record) processing. If such a data controller chooses not to notify in respect of the manual processing then he must, under paragraph (g) of the registrable particulars (below), state that notification does not extend to the manual records.

Transitional provisions exempt a data controller who is registered under the 1984 Act from the prohibition in s. 17(1) — see chapter 8, 'Effect of 1984 Act registration'.

REQUIRED INFORMATION

A data controller who wishes to be included in the register of data controllers maintained by the Commissioner must 'give a notification' under s. 18 of the Act (notification regulations will specify the precise form of the material to be supplied). The notification must specify:

(a)   the registrable particulars, and
(b)   a general description of the measures to be taken to ensure compliance with the seventh principle.

Section 16(1) provides that the registrable particulars of a data controller are:

(a)   his name and address,
(b)   the name and address of any representative of his,
(c)   a description of the personal data being or to be processed and the category of data subjects to which they relate,
(d)   a description of the purpose of processing,
(e)   a description of any intended recipients of the data,
(f)   a list of the countries outside the European Economic Area that will or might be in receipt of the data from the data controller, and
(g)   a statement (if relevant) of the fact that certain data processed by the data controller is of a type that is excluded from notification (see 'Prohibition on processing' above).

The address of the data controller should be the registered office (where the data controller is a company) or the principal place of business in the United Kingdom.

The seventh principle requires appropriate technical and organisational measures to be in place so as to ensure that the following do not occur to personal data:

(a)   unlawful or unauthorised processing; and
(b)   accidental loss, destruction or damage (see chapter 3 for further detail).

EXEMPTION FROM NOTIFICATION

Notification is not required in respect of any processing whose sole purpose is the maintenance of a public register (s. 17(4)). In addition the Secretary of State is expected to make regulations which exempt certain processing from the notification requirements. At the time of writing no such regulations exist. However, some advance indication of their likely content is gleanable from Article 18(2) of the Directive:

Member States may provide for the simplification of or exemption from notification only in the following cases and under the following conditions:
— where, for categories of processing operations which are unlikely, taking account of the data to be processed, to affect adversely the rights and freedoms of data subjects, they specify the purposes of the processing, the data or categories of data undergoing processing, the category or categories of data subject, the recipients or categories of recipient to whom the data are to be disclosed and the length of time the data are to be stored, and/or
— where the controller, in compliance with the national law which governs him, appoints a personal data protection official, responsible in particular:
for ensuring in an independent manner the internal application of the national provisions taken pursuant to this Directive,
for keeping the register of processing operations carried out by the controller, containing the items of information referred to in Article 21(2),
thereby ensuring that the rights and freedoms of the data subjects are unlikely to be adversely affected by the processing operations.

The regulations should therefore specify the precise conditions necessary for exemption and will concern only those cases which are unlikely to interfere with the rights and freedoms of data subjects. Alternatively exemption may be conferred where the data controller appoints a data protection supervisor (see below).

The processing of personal data must comply with the eight principles even if it is exempted from notification.

THE REGISTER

Section 19 requires the Commissioner to maintain a register of notifications by data controllers. The register will consist of the registrable particulars together with any other information required by the notification regulations. The fee that must accompany notification covers registration for an initial period only. Section 19(5) provides that this period is one year, but this is subject to change by notification regulations. A further fee is payable on the expiry of that period and each subsequent period.

The Commissioner must include in the register an entry in respect of each person who is exempt from the prohibition in s. 17(1) by virtue of sch. 16, para. 2 — see chapter 8, 'Effect of 1984 Act registration'.

Public inspection

The Commissioner is obliged to make the register open to the public for inspection at reasonable hours and free of charge. The register can be inspected at the premises of the Commissioner (Wyecliffe House, Water Lane, Wilmslow, Cheshire SK9 5AF) and is also available on the World Wide Web at http://www.open.gov.uk/dpr/dprhome.htm. The office of the Commissioner will normally provide photocopies of register entries by post free of charge.

NOTIFICATION OF CHANGES

Section 20 puts every registered data controller under a duty to inform the Commissioner of any change in:

(a)   the registrable particulars, or
(b)   the measures taken to comply with the seventh principle.

What will and will not constitute a change for these purposes is to be set out in the notification regulations.

Upon receiving notification of the alterations in the registrable particulars, the Commissioner must ensure that the register is updated to reflect the change (s. 20(4)).

Criminal offence

By virtue of s. 21(2), failure to notify the Commissioner of changes as required by s. 20 is a criminal offence. It is a defence for the person charged to show that he exercised all due diligence to comply with the duty.

ASSESSABLE PROCESSING

Section 22 provides that the Commissioner must, after receiving particulars from the data controller (either by way of initial notification or by a notification of changes), determine whether the processing to be undertaken by the data controller is assessable processing. If it is, then the Commissioner must inform the data controller of this fact within 28 days of receiving the particulars from the data controller. The Commissioner must also state whether the assessable processing is likely to comply with the provisions of the Act.

The Commissioner's 28-day time limit is extendible (once only) in special circumstances by a maximum of 14 days, at the option of the Commissioner by notice to the data controller. The Secretary of State may, by order, amend the time limit.

Assessable processing is defined in s. 22(1) to be processing that appears particularly likely:

(a)   to cause substantial damage or substantial distress to data subjects, or

(b)   otherwise significantly to prejudice the rights and freedoms of data subjects.

Section 22 requires the Secretary of State to specify, by order, the types of processing that will meet the above test. The Commissioner will be unable to make appropriate determinations until the assessable processing regulations have been made.

Processing which was already under way immediately before 24 October 1998 is not assessable processing for the purposes of s. 22 (sch. 8, para. 19).

Criminal Offence

Under s. 22(5) and (6) it is a criminal offence to carry on assessable processing after notification of such to the Commissioner unless either:

(a)   the period during which the Commissioner can notify the data controller whether the processing will comply with the Act (28 days unless extended by notice) has elapsed, or

(b)   before the end of the period in (a) the data controller has received a notice from the Commissioner stating the extent to which the Commissioner is of the opinion that the processing is likely or unlikely to comply with the provisions of the Act.

It is unclear from the statute whether, in option (b) above, the s. 22(6) offence will still apply to processing which the Commissioner states to be unlikely to comply with the provisions of the Act.

DATA PROTECTION SUPERVISORS

The Data Protection Act 1998 confers on the Secretary of State the power to make regulations concerning the appointment of data protection supervisors. Such persons would be employed by data controllers but be independent in respect of their data protection functions. The supervisor will monitor the data controller's data protection activity with a view to ensuring compliance with the legislation. The benefit to the data controller in making such an appointment is that the notification provisions will take effect in respect to it subject to certain modifications, which will be specified in the notification regulations.

DUTY OF DISCLOSURE

Section 24 imposes a duty on a data controller who chooses not to register with the Commissioner where notification is not compulsory because:

(a)   the only personal data being processed are manual data recorded as part of a relevant filing system (and the processing is not assessable processing); or

(b)   the only personal data being processed are part of an accessible record (and the processing is not assessable processing); or

(c)   notification regulations provide that processing of that description does not require notification.

The duty under s. 24 is that the data controller must, within 21 days of receiving a written request from any person, make the relevant particulars available in writing to that person free of charge. The relevant particulars are items (a) to (f) of the registrable particulars listed in s. 16(1) (see 'Required information' above). Thus lack of notification and hence lack of registration does not mean that a data controller will not be required to make the appropriate disclosure to a data subject.

The Secretary of State may provide exemptions from the operation of s. 24 in the notification regulations.

Criminal offence

It is a criminal offence to fail to comply with this duty of disclosure (s. 24(4)). It is a defence to show that all due diligence to comply was exercised by the defendant. Thus a non-negligent accidental failure to set out the relevant particulars fully should escape conviction.

DO I NEED TO NOTIFY?

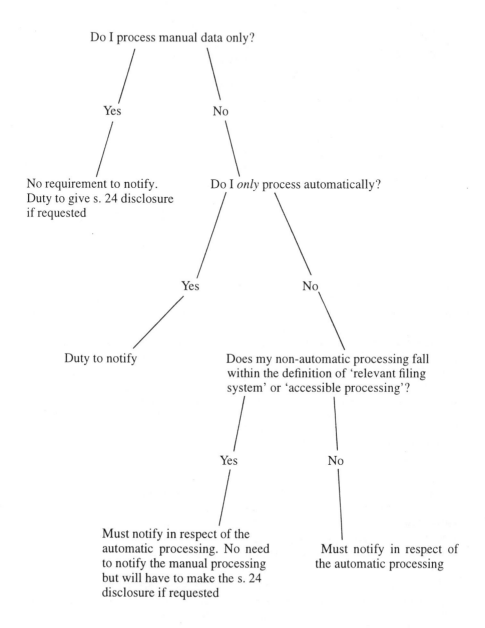

Do I process manual data only?

Yes

No

No requirement to notify. Duty to give s. 24 disclosure if requested

Do I *only* process automatically?

Yes

No

Duty to notify

Does my non-automatic processing fall within the definition of 'relevant filing system' or 'accessible processing'?

Yes

No

Must notify in respect of the automatic processing. No need to notify the manual processing but will have to make the s. 24 disclosure if requested

Must notify in respect of the automatic processing

Chapter 5
Exemptions

This chapter is divided into two parts. The first part deals with general and permanent exemptions from certain provisions of the Data Protection Act 1998. The second part looks at transitional exemptions, i.e., exemptions which are available for a limited period of time only.

PART 1   PERMANENT EXEMPTIONS

INTRODUCTION AND DEFINITIONS

Exemptions from certain provisions in the Data Protection Act 1998 exist for various purposes. The main exemptions appear in part IV of the statute. Various miscellaneous exemptions are listed in sch. 7. This part explains the exemptions in both part IV and sch. 7. Schedule 8 lists transitional exemptions — these are dealt with in part 2. Each of the exemptions authorises non-compliance with various of the statute's provisions. Table 5.1 on page 48 lists the provisions of the Act from which the data controller is exempt in respect of each exemption.

The detailed exemption provisions of the Act require an understanding of the definition of two key phrases which have been devised by the drafters of the legislation for ease of reference. Each refers to several of the provisions of the statute in respect of which an exemption might apply. They are 'the subject information provisions' and 'the non-disclosure provisions'.

The 'subject information provisions' are:

(a)   the right of the data subject to receive information relating to the identity of the data controller, the purpose of the processing and anything else necessary to ensure fairness (i.e., the first data protection principle to the extent to which it requires compliance with sch. 1, part II, para. 2), and

(b)   the right of access to personal data (i.e., the rights in s. 7).

The statute gives the subject information provisions special status by providing that any other rule of law that seeks to restrict the giving of the information specified shall not apply (s. 27(5)). The only restrictions that can exist are therefore the exemptions contained in the Act.

The 'non-disclosure provisions' means, to the extent t
the disclosure in question, the following:

(a)   the fair and lawful processing requiremen
principle (i.e., the first principle except the need to c

(b)   the second, third, fourth and fifth data prote

(c)   the right to prevent processing likely to cause u...

(d)   the right to rectification, blocking, erasure or destruction ...

In addition to those listed below, the Secretary of State is empowered to make
further exemptions from the subject information provisions and the non-disclosure
provisions.

	Provisions from which exempt
...al security	The data protection principles
	Rights of data subjects (part II)
	Notification provisions (part III)
	Enforcement (part V)
	Unlawful obtaining offence (s. 55)
Crime and taxation	First data protection principle (except sch. 2 and sch. 3)
	The subject access provisions in s. 7
	The non-disclosure provisions
Health, education and social work	The subject information provisions (regulations awaited)
Regulatory activity	The subject information provisions
Journalism, literature and art	The data protection principles (except the seventh)
	The subject access provisions in s. 7
	Right to prevent processing likely to cause damage or distress (s. 10)
	Rights in relation to automated decision-taking (s. 12)
	Right to rectification, blocking, erasure or destruction (s. 14(1) to (3))
Research, history and statistics	Certain aspects of the second and fifth data protection principles
	The subject access provisions in s. 7
Public inspection	The subject information provisions
	The fourth data protection principle
	Right to rectification, blocking, erasure or destruction (s. 14(1) to (3))
	The non-disclosure provisions
Corporate finance	The subject information provisions
Examination marks	Certain aspects of the subject access provisions in s. 7
Disclosures required by law	The non-disclosure provisions
Legal proceedings	The non-disclosure provisions
Domestic purposes	The data protection principles
	Rights of data subjects (part II)
	Notification provisions (part III)
Confidential references	The subject access provisions in s. 7
Armed forces	The subject information provisions
Judicial appointments and honours	The subject information provisions
Crown or Ministerial appointments	The subject information provisions
Management forecasts	The subject information provisions
Negotiations	The subject information provisions
Examination scripts	The subject access provisions in s. 7
Legal professional privilege	The subject information provisions
Self-incrimination	The subject access provisions in s. 7

Table 5.1

The remainder of this chapter will examine each of the exemptions in more detail.

NATIONAL SECURITY

Personal data are exempt from the following provisions of the Act where such an exemption is required for the purpose of 'safeguarding national security':

(a)   the data protection principles,
(b)   the rights of data subjects (part II),
(c)   the notification provisions (part III),
(d)   enforcement (part V),
(e)   the offence of unlawful obtaining (s. 55).

A Minister (who must be a member of the Cabinet, the Attorney-General or the Lord Advocate) may certify, under s. 28(2), that any specified processing is required for the purposes of safeguarding national security. The certificate may describe, in general terms, the personal data to which it relates and may be issued in anticipation of future processing. Any person directly affected by the certification may, by virtue of s. 28(4), appeal to the Tribunal against its application. The Tribunal will treat the appeal as if it was an application for judicial review, and will revoke the certificate where the Minister did not have reasonable grounds for its issue.

Any party to any proceedings under the Act concerning a generally worded certificate may appeal to the Tribunal on the basis that the Minister's certification does not cover the personal data in question. The decision of the Tribunal is conclusive (s. 28(6) and (7)). Any party wishing to challenge the authenticity of a certificate has the burden of proving that it is not a s. 28(2) certificate. A certified copy of a certificate is admissible in the same way as the original.

CRIME AND TAXATION

Section 29 gives an exemption to the processing of personal data for the following purposes:

(a)   the prevention or detection of crime,
(b)   the apprehension or prosecution of offenders, or
(c)   the assessment or collection of any tax or duty or of any imposition of a similar nature.

Such personal data are exempt from:

(a)   the first data protection principle (except sch. 2 and sch. 3),
(b)   the subject access provisions in s. 7.

Personal data which are processed with a view to compliance with a statutory function and which have been obtained from a person who possessed it for one of the purposes in (a) to (c) above are exempt from the subject information provisions.

Personal data are exempt from the non-disclosure provisions where the disclosure is for one of the purposes in (a) to (c) above and the application of those provisions would be likely to prejudice those purposes.

Where the data controller is a government department or local authority (or any other authority administering council tax or housing benefit) certain personal data are exempt from the subject access provisions in s. 7 so far as is necessary for the smooth running of a risk assessment system. The exempt personal data for this purpose are defined in s. 29(4) those which:

(a)   consist of a classification applied to the data subject as part of a system of risk assessment which is operated by the authority for either of the following purposes—

(i)   the assessment or collection of any tax or duty or any imposition of a similar nature, or

(ii)   the prevention or detection of crime, or apprehension or prosecution of offenders, where the offence concerned involves any unlawful claim for any payment out of, or any unlawful application of, public funds [including funds provided by any Community institution: s. 29(5)], and

(b)   are processed for either of those purposes.

HEALTH, EDUCATION AND SOCIAL WORK

Section 30 gives power to the Secretary of State to make provision for exemption from the subject information provisions (or modification of those provisions) for personal data which are processed for health, education and social-work purposes. Regulations are expected specifically in relation to personal data concerning:

(a)   the physical or mental health or condition of the data subject,

(b)   current or ex-pupils at a school where the data controller is the proprietor or a teacher, and

(c)   current or ex-further education students where the data controller is a Scottish education authority.

Additionally the Secretary of State may exempt personal data from the subject information provisions (or modify them) where the personal data are both:

(a)   processed by government departments or local authorities or by voluntary organisations or other bodies designated by or under the order, and

(b)   processed in the course of social work in relation to any individual.

But s. 30(3) prevents exemption or modification for these purposes unless the application of the provisions as originally enacted would be likely to prejudice the carrying out of social work.

REGULATORY ACTIVITY

Certain functions are given special status by s. 31, which provides that personal data processed for the purpose of such functions will be exempt from the subject information provisions where compliance with those provisions would prejudice those functions.

The section provides an exhaustive list of the functions to which the exemption relates. Examples are any relevant function which is designed:

(a)   for protecting members of the public against—

(i)   financial loss due to dishonesty, malpractice or other seriously improper conduct by, or the unfitness or incompetence of, persons concerned in the provision of banking, insurance, investment or other financial services or in the management of bodies corporate,

(ii)   financial loss due to the conduct of discharged or undischarged bankrupts, or

(iii)   dishonesty, malpractice or other seriously improper conduct by, or the unfitness or incompetence of, persons authorised to carry on any profession or other activity,

(b)   to protect charities against misconduct or mismanagement;
(c)   to protect the property of charities from loss or misapplication;
(d)   for the recovery of the property of charities;
(e)   for ensuring the health and safety of persons at work;
(f)   to protect non-employees against health and safety risks arising out of the activities of persons at work.

A relevant function is defined in s. 31(3) as:

(a)   any function conferred on any person by virtue of a statute,
(b)   any function of the Crown or a Minister or government department, or
(c)   any other public function which is exercised in the public interest.

Section 31(4) lists further exemptions (from the subject information provisions) for personal data which are processed for the protection of the public by persons such as:

(a)   the Parliamentary Commissioner for Administration,
(b)   the Local Administration Commissioners for England, Wales and Scotland,
(c)   the Welsh Administration Ombudsman,
(d)   the Assembly Ombudsman for Northern Ireland,
(e)   the Northern Ireland Commissioner for Complaints,
(f)   the Health Service Commissioner for England, Wales and Scotland.

Section 31(5) exempts from the subject information provisions personal data processed by the Director General of Fair Trading for the purpose of:

(a)   protecting members of the public against conduct which may adversely affect their interests by persons carrying on a business,
(b)   regulating agreements or conduct which have as their object or effect the prevention, restriction or distortion of competition in connection with any commercial activity, or
(c)   regulating conduct on the part of one or more undertakings which amounts to the abuse of a dominant position in a market

to the extent to which the application of those provisions to the data would be likely to prejudice the proper discharge of the duties.

JOURNALISM, LITERATURE AND ART

Data protection legislation is founded in a desire to preserve the right of privacy. Although there is no such right in English law, this legislation and other statutes in the pipeline in 1998 were expected to create substantial privacy rights. However, media proved to be a powerful lobby during the course of the creation of the legislation and the so-called media exemption in the Data Protection Act 1998, s. 32, preserves, at least in part, the freedom of the press.

Journalists invariably hold on computers personal data on living individuals. In many cases this is sensitive personal data within the meaning of the Act, being information relating to, for example, a person's racial origin, political opinion or sex life. By virtue of this exemption, none of the conditions for the processing of sensitive personal data in sch. 2 apply to the media. Investigative journalism would clearly be hampered if the consent of the data subject was a requirement of processing.

The following provisions of the Act will not apply to the media where the exemption operates:

(a)   the data protection principles (except the seventh),
(b)   the subject access provisions in s. 7,
(c)   right to prevent processing likely to cause damage or distress (s. 10),
(d)   rights in relation to automated decision-taking (s. 12),
(e)   the transitional rights in s. 12A (see chapter 2, 'Transitional rights'),
(f)   right to rectification, blocking, erasure or destruction (s. 14(1) to (3)).

To benefit from the exemption personal data must be processed for the 'special purposes' and each of the following three prerequisites must be satisfied:

(a)   the processing must be undertaken with a view to the publication by any person of any journalistic, literary or artistic material,
(b)   the data controller must reasonably believe that, having regard in particular to the special importance of the public interest in freedom of expression, publication would be in the public interest, and
(c)   the data controller must reasonably believe that, in all the circumstances, compliance with the provision in question is incompatible with the special purposes.

The 'special purposes' are defined in s. 3 as meaning any one or more of the following:

(a)   the purposes of journalism,
(b)   artistic purposes,
(c)   literary purposes.

In considering whether the data controller reasonably believes the publication to be in the public interest he may have regard to his compliance with the provisions of 'any relevant code of practice'. In the case of newspaper journalists and editors the relevant code will be that of the Press Complaints Commission. Television broadcasters and programme makers outside the BBC will need to consult the ITC's code. Any such code must be designated by the Secretary of State as relevant for the purposes of this section.

Section 32(4) seems to prevent so-called gagging orders within 24 hours prior to publication by providing that proceedings against a data controller under any of the provisions to which the exemption relates will be stayed if the relevant personal data are being processed:

(a)   only for the special purposes, and
(b)   with a view to the publication of special purposes material which had not, excluding the 24-hour period prior to the proceedings, previously been published by the data controller.

The stay will remain in place until either the Commissioner makes a determination (under s. 45) that the personal data are not being processed in compliance with (a) and (b) above or the data controller withdraws his claim to have complied with (a) and (b) above. For further detail on the s. 45 determination procedure see chapter 6, 'Special information notice'.

RESEARCH, HISTORY AND STATISTICS

Those engaged in historical and other research, and in the preparation of certain statistics, will be able to escape some of the provisions of the Data Protection Act 1998, under s. 33 of the Act. This exemption relates to personal data which are processed 'only for research purposes'. 'Research purposes' is not defined in the Act but is stated to include statistical or historical purposes (s. 33(1)). A disclosure of personal data to any person for research purposes does not prevent the exemptions from applying, nor does a disclosure to a data subject or a person acting on his or her behalf. The research exemptions concern the following provisions of the Act:

(a)   the second data protection principle,
(b)   the fifth data protection principle,
(c)   the subject access provisions in s. 7.

The second data protection principle requires that data must not be processed in a manner which is incompatible with the purpose for which it was obtained. Section 33(2) provides that the processing of personal data for research purposes will not breach the second principle if the processing complies with certain 'relevant conditions' (see below). Further, personal data processed (in compliance with the same conditions) for research purposes can be kept indefinitely, notwithstanding the provisions against the keeping of 'old' data in the fifth principle.

An exemption from the subject access provisions in s. 7 is available for personal data which are processed for research purposes and the processing complies with the relevant conditions where 'the results of the research or any resulting statistics are not made available in a form which identifies data subjects or any of them' (s. 33(4)).

The relevant conditions mentioned in the three exemptions above are negatively defined in s. 33(1) as follows:

(a)   that the data are not processed to support measures or decisions with respect to particular individuals, and

(b)   that the data are not processed in such a way that substantial damage or substantial distress is, or is likely to be, caused to any data subject.

See further transitional exemptions for historical research in part 2 of this chapter.

PUBLIC INSPECTION

If a data controller is obliged by statute to make any disclosure of personal data to the public (whether by charging a fee or not) then the personal data are exempt from the following provisions:

(a)   the subject information provisions,
(b)   the fourth data protection principle,
(c)   the right to rectification, blocking, erasure or destruction (s. 14(1) to (3)),
(d)   the transitional rights in s. 12A (see chapter 2, 'Transitional rights'),
(e)   the non-disclosure provisions.

CORPORATE FINANCE

This exemption, contained in sch. 7, para. 6, concerns a corporate finance service, which is defined as:

a service consisting in:
   (a)   underwriting in respect of issues of, or the placing of issues of, any instrument,
   (b)   advice to undertakings on capital structure, industrial strategy and related matters and advice and service relating to mergers and the purchase of undertakings, or
   (c)   services relating to such underwriting as is mentioned in paragraph (a).

The exemption is designed to ensure that the market price or value of financial instruments, such as stocks, futures or annuities, is unaffected by knowledge of any dealings. Personal data processed for the purpose of a corporate finance service are exempt from the subject information provisions where the application of those provisions could affect the price of any instrument, or where the data controller reasonably believes an instrument could be so affected. The provisions cover both existing instruments and those to be created. Where the data are not exempt by virtue of the above, they nevertheless will benefit from a further exemption where required to safeguard an important economic interest of the United Kingdom.

In order for the exemption to operate, the corporate finance service must be provided by a specific type of person. The list of relevant persons appears in sch. 7, para. 6(3), and includes persons authorised to provide services under certain provisions of the Financial Services Act 1986 and certain European investment firms.

EXAMINATION MARKS

Paragraph 8 of sch. 7 modifies the time limit for compliance with the subject access provisions where the personal data consist of examination results.

Where personal data are processed for the purpose of determining examination results (or any consequence of such determination) the s. 7 time limits are extended. If the relevant day (commonly, the day the data controller receives the request for subject access — see chapter 2, 'Basic rights of access') falls before the day of the announcement of the examination results then the time period for compliance is extended until the earlier of:

(a)   the end of five months from the relevant day, or
(b)   the end of 40 days from the date of the announcement.

In certain cases the above provisions will inevitably result in a request under s. 7 being complied with after the expiry of the normal s. 7 time limits. Where this occurs the data supplied must not only be the data relevant to the date of the request but also must take account of any alterations in the data from that date until actual compliance.

OTHER EXEMPTIONS

This section lists further miscellaneous exemptions.

Disclosures required by law

Where the disclosure of personal data is required by law, whether statute, case law or court order, those personal data are exempt from the non-disclosure provisions (s. 35(1)).

Legal proceedings

Personal data are exempt from the non-disclosure provisions where the disclosure in question is necessary for the purpose of legal proceedings or for the obtaining of legal advice or for establishing, exercising or defending legal rights (s. 35(2)).

Domestic purposes

Personal data processed as part of household or domestic activities should not be subject to a rigid data protection regime. A Christmas card list, for example, would come under this exemption. Section 36 gives such personal data an exemption from the following provisions of the statute:

(a)   the data protection principles,
(b)   the rights of data subjects (part II),
(c)   the notification provisions (part III).

Confidential references

The statutory provisions recognise the importance to be attached to the confidential nature of references (sch. 7, para. 1). The value of an employer's reference would be diminished if the subject of the reference was able to obtain a copy of the personal data it contained.

Personal data are exempt from the subject access provisions in s. 7 if they are included as part of a confidential reference given or to be given by the data controller for the purpose of:

(a)   the education, training or employment, or prospective education, training or employment, of the data subject,
(b)   the appointment, or prospective appointment, of the data subject to any office, or
(c)   the provision, or prospective provision, by the data subject of any service.

Armed forces

Personal data are exempt from the subject information provisions to the extent that those provisions are likely to prejudice the 'combat effectiveness' of the armed forces of the Crown (sch. 7, para. 2).

Judicial appointments and honours

An exemption from the subject information provisions is available in respect of personal data processed for determining the suitability of a person for appointment as a judge or Queen's Counsel or for the conferring of any honour by the Crown.

Crown or Ministerial appointments

The Secretary of State is empowered to produce subject information exemptions for personal data which are processed for the purpose of assessing the suitability of any person for appointment as a Minister or other government employee. No such exemptions exist at the time of writing.

Management forecasts

Where it would be of assistance to the data controller in 'the conduct of any business or other activity', personal data are exempt from the subject information provisions (to the extent that those provisions would be prejudicial to that business or other activity) where processed for the following purposes:

(a)   management forecasting, or
(b)   management planning (sch. 7, para. 5).

Negotiations

Where the data controller makes a record of his intentions in respect of negotiations with a data subject, then that record is exempt from the subject information provisions to the extent that those provisions would be likely to prejudice the negotiation (sch. 7, para. 7).

Examination scripts

In certain circumstances the information given by students in examinations will consist of personal data. The exemption in sch. 7, para. 9, provides that anything written down by candidates in a professional or academic examination is exempt from the subject access provisions in s. 7.

Legal professional privilege

Personal data are exempt from the subject information provisions in so far as they consist of material for which legal professional privilege can be claimed.

Self-incrimination

A data controller is exempted from complying with any request or order for information under s. 7 where such compliance would expose the controller to proceedings for any offence. The exemption relates to all criminal offences except offences under the Data Protection Act 1998 itself. But if a controller does make information available to another under s. 7, the information cannot be used in any criminal proceedings against that controller for an offence under the 1998 Act (sch. 7, para, 11).

PART 2   TRANSITIONAL EXEMPTIONS

INTRODUCTION AND DEFINITIONS

This part looks at certain exemptions which result from limited-duration modifications to the Act — all of which are contained in Schedule 8. The two most important dates for these purposes are 23 October 2001 (the end of the *first transitional period*) and 23 October 2007 (the end of the *second transitional period*). The first transitional period will begin when Schedule 8 is brought into force (this is expected to be in early 1999). The second transitional period commences on 24 October 2001.

The exemptions in Schedule 8 relate to 'eligible data'. Personal data are eligible data if they are subject to processing which was already under way immediately before 24 October 1998. There is no definition of the phrase 'already under way' in the Act. Secondary legislation, expected in 1999 may clarify the operation of this provision.

Eligible automated data

'Eligible automated data' means eligible data which consists of information which is being processed by means of equipment operating automatically in response to instructions given for that purpose or which is recorded with the intention that it should be so processed (this is the first two parts of the definition of 'data' in s. 1(1)). During the first transitional period eligible automated data are not to be regarded as 'processed' unless the processing is by reference to the data subject.

In addition to the specific exemptions listed in the remainder of this chapter, eligible automated data are exempt from the following provisions of the Act during the *first transitional period*:

(a)   the first data protection principle in so far as it requires compliance with sch. 2 and sch. 3 (this exemption does not remove the obligation on the data controller to ensure that the processing is fair),

(b)   that part of the seventh data protection principle which requires any processing carried out by a data processor on behalf of a data controller to be carried out under certain contractual provisions (see chapter 3),

(c)   the eighth data protection principle (but any transfer of data abroad must comply with the fairness requirement in the first principle),

(d)   those parts of the subject access provisions (s. 7) which require the data subject to be given descriptions of the data, its purpose and likely recipients, the source of the data and the logic involved in automated decision-taking,

(e)   the right in s. 10 to prevent processing likely to cause damage or distress (this does not remove the obligation on the data controller to process fairly as required by the first principle),

(f)   the right in s. 11 to prevent direct marketing processing (such processing must be fair as required by the first principle),

(g)   the right to request that a decision affecting the data subject is not taken solely by automated means (s. 12),

(h)   the right to compensation (s. 13) except where relating to:

(i)   a contravention of the fourth data protection principle,
(ii)   a disclosure without the consent of the data controller,
(iii)   loss or destruction of data without the consent of the data controller, or
(iv)   processing for the special purposes.

Eligible manual data

Processing which was already under way immediately before 24 October 1998 is not assessable processing for the purposes of s. 22 (sch. 8, para. 19).

'Eligible manual data' means eligible data not falling within the definition of eligible automated data (i.e., personal data which are recorded or intended to be recorded as part of a relevant filing system or which forms part of an accessible record — see chapter 2, 'Initial definitions').

MANUAL DATA

Subject to the two exceptions below, eligible manual data are exempt from the following provisions of the Act during the *first transitional period*:

(a)   the data protection principles,

(b)   part II of the Act (the data subject's rights of access, rights to prevent processing and rights to rectification, blocking, erasure, destruction and compensation),

(c)   part III of the Act (the notification provisions).

The two types of data which do not benefit from the above transitional exemption are:

(a)   data forming part of an accessible record, and
(b)   data held by a credit reference agency (sch. 8, para. 3).

Data forming part of an accessible record

Eligible manual data forming part of an accessible record (whether or not processing was already under way on 24 October 1998) are exempt from the following provisions during the *first transitional period*:

(a)   the data protection principles, except the sixth principle so far as relating to ss. 7 and 12A,

(b)   part II of the Act, except ss. 7, 12A and 15,

(c)   part III of the Act.

Credit reference agency

Eligible manual data which consist of information relevant to the financial standing of the data subject and in respect of which the data controller is a credit reference agency (see definition in chapter 2) are exempt from the following provisions during the *first transitional period*:

(a)   the data protection principles, except the sixth principle so far as relating to ss. 7 and 12A,

(b)   part II of the Act, except ss. 7, 12A and 15

(c)   part III of the Act.

Second transitional period

Eligible manual data (other than data which are processed only for the purpose of historical research) which were held immediately before 24 October 1998 and any other personal data forming part of an accessible record are exempt from the following provisions of the Act during the *second transitional period*:

(a)   the first data protection principle except to the extent to which it requires compliance with sch. 1, part II, para. 2.

(b)   the second data protection principle,

(c)   the third data protection principle,

(d)   the fourth data protection principle,

(e)   the fifth data protection principle,

(f)   the rights in respect of court orders for rectification, blocking, erasure and destruction under s. 14(1) to (3).

PAYROLLS

Under sch. 8, para. 6, eligible automated data processed for the purpose of calculating salaries, wages or pensions are exempt (provided that the processing was done only for one or more of those purposes or the data controller took reasonable steps to ensure that was the case) from the following provisions during the *first transitional period*:

(a)   the data protection principles,

(b)   part II of the Act,

(c)   part III of the Act.

Data which are processed only for the above purposes may be disclosed:

(a)   to any person (other than the data controller) by whom the remuneration or pensions in question are payable,

(b)   for the purpose of obtaining actuarial advice,

(c)   for the purpose of giving information as to the persons in any employment or office for use in medical research into the health of, or injuries suffered by, persons engaged in particular occupations or working in particular places or areas,

(d)   if the data subject (or a person acting on his or her behalf) has requested or consented to the disclosure of the data either generally or in the circumstances in which the disclosure in question is made,

(e)   if the person making the disclosure has reasonable grounds for believing that the disclosure falls within paragraph (d), or

(f)   for the purpose of audit or where the disclosure is for the purpose only of giving information about the data controller's financial affairs.

ACCOUNTS

Eligible automated data processed for the purpose of keeping business or other accounts or keeping records of purchases, sales or other transactions for the purpose of making or receiving payment or of making management forecasts are exempt (provided that the processing was done only for one or more of those purposes or the data controller took reasonable steps to ensure that was the case) from the following provisions during the *first transitional period*:

(a)   the data protection principles,

(b)   part II of the Act,

(c)   part III of the Act.

Data which are processed only for the above purposes may be disclosed for the purpose of audit or where the disclosure is for the purpose only of giving information about the data controller's financial affairs.

UNINCORPORATED MEMBERS' CLUBS

Subject to the conditions below, eligible automated data processed by an unincorporated members' club are exempt from the following of the Act's provisions during the *first transitional period*:

(a)   the data protection principles,

(b)   part II of the Act,

(c)   part III of the Act.

This transitional exemption does not apply unless the data subject has indicated to the club that there is no objection to the processing of his or her personal data. If the data subject does object then the processing cannot benefit from the exemption.

A further condition on the operation of the exemption is that the data must not be disclosed unless one of the following apply:

(a)   the data subject (or a person acting on his or her behalf) has requested or consented to the disclosure of the data either generally or in the circumstances in which the disclosure in question is made, or

(b)   the person making the disclosure has reasonable grounds for believing that the disclosure falls within paragraph (a).

Any disclosure otherwise than in accordance with (a) or (b) above will not result in the loss of the transitional exemption where the data controller is able to show that reasonable care was taken to prevent the disclosure.

MAILING LISTS

Subject to the conditions below, eligible automated data consisting only of names, addresses and other particulars necessary for ensuring delivery and processed only for the purposes of distribution of information or articles are exempt from the following of the Act's provisions during the *first transitional period*:

(a)   the data protection principles,
(b)   part II of the Act,
(c)   part III of the Act.

This transitional exemption does not apply unless the data subject has indicated to the data controller that there is no objection to the processing of his or her personal data. If the data subject does object then the processing cannot benefit from the exemption.

A further condition on the operation of the exemption is that the data must not be disclosed unless one of the following applies:

(a)   the data subject (or a person acting on his or her behalf) has requested or consented to the disclosure of the data either generally or in the circumstances in which the disclosure in question is made,

(b)   the person making the disclosure has reasonable grounds for believing that the disclosure falls within paragraph (a),

(c)   disclosure would be permitted by any other provision of sch. 8, part II, if the provision giving the mailing list exemption were included among the non-disclosure provisions.

Any disclosure otherwise than in accordance with (a) or (b) above will not result in the loss of the transitional exemption where the data controller is able to show that reasonable care was taken to prevent the disclosure.

BACK-UP DATA

Eligible automated data which are processed only for the purpose of replacing other data in the event of the data being lost, destroyed or impaired are exempt from the subject access provisions in s. 7 during the *first transitional period*.

HISTORICAL RESEARCH

Both eligible manual and eligible automated data processed for the purposes of historical research are exempt from certain provisions of the Act after 23 October 2001. The benefit of this exemption (in the case of both manual and automated data) will not be lost merely because the data concerned are disclosed:

(a)   to any person, for the purpose of historical research only,

(b)   to the data subject or a person acting on his behalf,

(c)   at the request, or with the consent, of the data subject or a person acting on his behalf, or

(d)   in circumstances in which the person making the disclosure has reasonable grounds for believing that the disclosure falls within paragraph (a), (b) or (c).

A further condition of the operation of the exemption (for both manual and automated data) is that the processing must be in compliance with the 'relevant conditions'. These conditions are the same as the relevant conditions in s. 33, which relate to the permanent exemptions for research, history and statistics, i.e.:

(a)   that the data are not processed to support measures or decisions with respect to particular individuals, and

(b)   that the data are not processed in such a way that substantial damage or substantial distress is, or is likely to be, caused to any data subject.

Manual data

Eligible manual data which are processed only for the purpose of historical research in compliance with the relevant conditions (see above) are exempt from the following provisions of the Act *after 23 October 2001*:

(a)   the first data protection principle except to the extent to which it requires compliance with sch. 1, part II, para. 2,

(b)   the second data protection principle,

(c)   the third data protection principle,

(d)   the fourth data protection principle,

(e)   the fifth data protection principle,

(f)   the rights in respect of court orders for rectification, blocking, erasure and destruction under s. 14(1) to (3).

Automated data

Eligible automated data which are processed only for the purpose of historical research in compliance with the relevant conditions (see above) are exempt from the following provision of the Act *after 23 October 2001*:

(a)   the first data protection principle in so far as it requires compliance with the conditions in sch. 2 and sch. 3.

Where such data are processed otherwise than by reference to the data subject they are also exempt from the following provisions:

(a)   the first data protection principle except to the extent to which it requires compliance with sch. 1, part II, para. 2,

(b)   the second data protection principle,

(c)   the third data protection principle,

(d)   the fourth data protection principle,

(e)   the fifth data protection principle,

(f)   the rights in respect of court orders for rectification, blocking, erasure and destruction under s. 14(1) to (3).

Chapter 6
Enforcement

INTRODUCTION

Part V of the Data Protection Act 1998 provides methods by which the Commissioner can seek to ensure that data controllers comply with the provisions of the Act. The Commissioner's powers revolve around serving notices on data controllers. Information and special information notices require data controllers to supply information to the Commissioner, while enforcement notices require data controllers to comply with measures which they list. It is a criminal offence to fail to respond appropriately to any of the notices.

Obviously a notice is unlikely to be served on a data controller unless the Commissioner has received some information concerning a potential compliance issue. This may occur in a number of ways. Section 42, for example, provides that any person may apply to the Commissioner for an assessment of whether any processing concerning him or her is being carried out lawfully. The mechanics of such a request are examined below.

The processing of special purposes material is examined here in some detail as it gives rise to a more complex notice procedure.

REQUEST FOR ASSESSMENT

Any person who believes that he or she is being directly affected by the processing of personal data may apply to the Commissioner for an assessment of whether that processing is being carried out in compliance with the Act (s. 42). Such a request will usually be made where the person concerned feels that the processing is being carried out in contravention of the Act. The request should contain details of the applicant's name and of any other relevant information sufficient to enable the Commissioner to identify the processing in question. In determining the appropriate manner in which to make an assessment, the Commissioner will consider all relevant information including:

(a) the extent to which the request appears to her to raise a matter of substance,

(b) any undue delay in making the request, and

(c) whether or not the person making the request is entitled to make an application under s. 7 in respect of the personal data in question.

Section 7 contains the provisions which enable a data subject to gain access to information concerning personal data held by a data controller (see chapter 2).

Section 42(4) requires the Commissioner to notify the applicant whether an assessment has been made and to inform the applicant of any view formed or action taken as a result of the request. In determining the appropriateness of the Commissioner's response under s. 42(4) the Commissioner shall bear in mind the extent to which the personal data concerned are exempt from the provisions of s. 7. For a discussion of the exemptions see chapter 5.

INFORMATION NOTICE

Under s. 43 the Commissioner may serve a document, known as an information notice, on any data controller requiring the data controller to furnish certain information to the Commissioner within a time limit specified in the notice. The purpose of the notice is to allow the Commissioner to gather sufficient information to determine whether the data controller is processing in contravention of the statutory provisions.

Service of an information notice on any particular data controller must be for one of two reasons:

(a)   that the Commissioner has received an application for an assessment under s. 42 (see above), or

(b)   that the Commissioner reasonably requires the information requested in the information notice for the purpose of determining whether the data controller has complied, or is complying, with the data protection principles.

If the Commissioner has served an information notice following an application for an assessment, she must inform the data controller of that fact and must specify the particular processing in question. In all other cases the information notice must state why the Commissioner regards the information requested as being relevant for the purpose of determining whether the data controller is complying with the data protection principles.

In every case the information notice must contain particulars of the s. 48 rights of appeal to the Tribunal (s. 43(3)). See below for further information on the appeal process.

Time limit for compliance

The time limit imposed on a data controller by the Commissioner for compliance with the information notice starts to run from the day the notice is served. In most cases it cannot expire before the day on which the rights of appeal against the notice elapse (see below) and, where an appeal is brought, will not expire until the determination or withdrawal of the appeal. Exceptionally, and where the Commissioner requires the information as a matter of urgency, the time limit specified in the notice can be shorter than the above but must not be less than seven days. In this event the Commissioner must make a statement why she considers the matter to be urgent. There is a right of appeal to the tribunal against the Commissioner's decision to include such a statement and against its effect (see below, 'Appeals').

Section 43(9) allows the Commissioner to withdraw (in writing) an information notice. Compliance is not required after such a withdrawal.

Exemptions from compliance

A person may choose not to comply with an information notice where compliance would reveal one or more of the following:

(a)   the content of any communication between a lawyer and his or her client where the subject of such communication is advice in respect of the client's rights, obligations or liabilities under the Act,

(b)   the content of any communication between a lawyer and his or her client, or between a lawyer or his or her client and any other person, made in connection with or in contemplation of proceedings (including proceedings before the Tribunal) under the Act, or

(c)   the commission by that person of an actionable criminal offence (except a criminal offence under the Act).

Special purposes

Section 46(3) prevents the Commissioner from serving an information notice on a data controller which relates to processing for the special purposes (see chapter 5, 'Journalism, literature and art') unless the Commissioner has made a determination (under s. 45) that the personal data:

(a)   are not being processed only for the special purposes, or

(b)   are not being processed with a view to the publication by any person of any journalistic, literary or artistic material which has not previously been published by the data controller.

Criminal offences

It is an offence to fail to comply with an information notice (s. 47(1)). It is a defence to show that the accused exercised all due diligence to comply with the notice.

Further, it is an offence to make a false statement (knowingly or recklessly) in response to an information notice (s. 47(2)).

SPECIAL INFORMATION NOTICE

The exemption relating to processing for the special purposes, i.e., for journalistic, literary or artistic purposes, was discussed in chapter 5. It is a significant exemption which preserves freedom of speech and writing for those who publish public interest material. The Commissioner's powers under the special information notice procedure exist to ensure that the exemption is used only in appropriate circumstances.

Where the Commissioner wishes to ascertain whether personal data are being processed only for the special purposes or with a view to publication of journalistic, literary or artistic material which has not previously been published by the data controller (i.e., the grounds for a stay under s. 32(4) — see chapter 5, 'Journalism, literature and art') she may serve a notice (a 'special information notice') on the data controller which requests the data controller to supply certain information.

By s. 44(1) a special information notice may only be served where the Commissioner:

(a)   has received a request for an assessment under s. 42, or

(b)   has reasonable grounds for suspecting that, in a case in which proceedings have been stayed under s. 32, the personal data to which the proceedings relate:

(i)   are not being processed only for the special purposes, or

(ii)   are not being processed with a view to the publication by any person of any journalistic, literary or artistic material which has not previously been published by the data controller.

The notice must state the grounds upon which it is served, the time limit for compliance and particulars of the rights of appeal conferred by s. 48 (see below). The prerequisite of either a request for assessment or a stay should mean that a special information notice is a relatively rarely used device.

Time limit for compliance

The time limit imposed on a data controller by the Commissioner for compliance with a special information notice starts to run from the day the notice is served. Subject to the limited exception below it cannot expire before the day on which the rights of appeal against the notice elapse and, where an appeal is brought, will not expire until the determination or withdrawal of the appeal. Exceptionally, and where the Commissioner requires the information as a matter of urgency, the time limit specified in the notice can be shorter than the above but must not be less than seven days. In this event the Commissioner must state why she considers the matter to be urgent. There is a right of appeal to the tribunal against the Commissioner's decision to include such a statement and against its effect (see below, 'Appeals').

A special information notice may be cancelled by the Commissioner after it has been served (s. 44(10)). Compliance is not required after such a cancellation.

Exemptions from compliance

A person may choose not to comply with a special information notice where compliance would reveal one or more of the following:

(a)   the content of any communication between a lawyer and his or her client where the subject of such communication is advice in respect of the client's rights, obligations or liabilities under the Act,

(b)   the content of any communication between a lawyer and his or her client, or between a lawyer or his or her client and any other person, made in connection with or in contemplation of proceedings (including proceedings before the Tribunal) under the Act, or

(c)   the commission by that person of an actionable criminal offence (except a criminal offence under the Act).

Determination by the Commissioner

Under s. 45 the Commissioner may, at any time, make a determination in writing to the data controller that certain specified processing is not being carried out only for the special purposes or with a view to publication of journalistic, literary or artistic material not previously published by the data controller. This will usually be done where the Commissioner has served a special information notice but is not limited to such cases. The purpose of such a determination is to allow the Commissioner to serve an enforcement notice — one of the prerequisites for serving an enforcement notice in respect of processing for the special purposes is the service by the Commissioner of a s. 45 determination on the data controller (for further detail see below, 'Enforcement notice — Special purposes').

Notice of a determination under s. 45 must be given to the data controller together with a statement of the rights of appeal covered by s. 48. The determination will not take effect until the end of the period in which an appeal can be brought. Where an appeal is brought the determination will have no effect until after the conclusion or withdrawal of the appeal.

Criminal offences

It is an offence to fail to comply with a special information notice (s. 47(1)). It is a defence to show that the defendant exercised all due diligence to comply with the notice.

Further, it is an offence to make a false statement (knowingly or recklessly) in response to a special information notice (s. 47(2)).

ENFORCEMENT NOTICE

Where the Commissioner is satisfied that a data controller has contravened or is contravening any of the data protection principles she may serve on the data controller a notice (an 'enforcement notice') requiring the data controller to take specific steps to rectify the contravention or to refrain from processing certain specified personal data (s. 40(1)). An enforcement notice is more likely to be served in cases where the contravention in question is causing (or is likely to cause) a person damage or distress.

Where the enforcement notice requires the data controller to rectify, block, erase or destroy any personal data the Commissioner may require the data controller to notify third parties of that rectification, blocking, erasure or destruction. The same is true where the Commissioner is satisfied that personal data which have been rectified, blocked, erased or destroyed had been processed in contravention of any of the data protection principles. In each case the requirement to notify third parties will not be imposed where this is not reasonably practicable (e.g., where there are a large number of such persons).

An enforcement notice which is concerned with a contravention of the fourth data protection principle (the obligation to keep personal data accurate and up to date) may, in addition to requiring the rectification, blocking, erasure or destruction of inaccurate personal data, impose a similar requirement in respect of any expression of opinion which appears to be based on the inaccurate data (s. 40(3)). Where, in the case of such a fourth principle enforcement notice the data accurately portray information conveyed to the data controller by the data subject or a third party, the enforcement notice may require the data controller either:

(a) to rectify, block, erase or destroy any inaccurate data and any other data containing an expression of opinion, and

(b) to take specified steps to check the accuracy of the data and (if relevant) to supplement the data with a statement reflecting the data subject's view of the inaccuracy of the data.

Every enforcement notice must contain a list of the data protection principles that are alleged to have been contravened and the grounds for that belief. The time limit for compliance should be given, along with a statement of the rights of appeal under s. 48.

An enforcement notice may be cancelled or varied by the Commissioner in writing to the data controller (s. 41(1)). A data controller who has received an enforcement notice may apply in writing to the Commissioner for the cancellation or variation of the notice. This may be done only where a change of circumstances of the data controller means that some or all of the requirements of the notice need not be complied with to ensure compliance with the data protection principles and only where the time limit for the bringing of an appeal has expired (s. 41(2)). An appeal is available against the decision of the Commissioner not to allow an application under s. 41(2) (see below, 'Appeals').

Time limit for compliance

The time limit imposed on a data controller by the Commissioner for compliance with an enforcement notice starts to run from the day the notice is served. Subject to the limited exception below it cannot expire before the day on which the rights of appeal against the notice elapse and, where an appeal is brought, will not expire until the determination or withdrawal of the appeal. Where the Commissioner requires the information as a matter of urgency, the time limit specified in the notice can be shorter than the above but must not be less than seven days. In this event the Commissioner must state why she considers the matter to be urgent. There is a right of appeal to the Tribunal against the Commissioner's decision to include such a statement and against its effect (see below, 'Appeals').

Special purposes

Section 46(1) prevents the Commissioner from serving an enforcement notice on a data controller which relates to processing for the special purposes unless the court has granted leave for the notice to be served and the Commissioner has made a determination (under s. 45) that the personal data:

(a) are not being processed only for the special purposes, or

(b) are not being processed with a view to the publication by any person of any journalistic, literary or artistic material which has not previously been published by the data controller.

The court will not grant leave for this purpose unless it is satisfied that the Commissioner has reason to suspect that the contravention of the data protection principles in question is of substantial public importance (s. 46(2)(a)). Additionally the court must be satisfied that the data controller has been given notice of the application for leave, which will not be necessary where the case is one of urgency (s. 46(2)(b)).

Criminal offence

It is an offence to fail to comply with an enforement notice (s. 47(1)). It is a defence to show that the defendant exercised all due diligence to comply with the notice.

APPEALS

Safeguards on the operation of powers by the Commissioner allow a data controller to appeal against certain decisions and procedures. Section 48 confers the following types of appeal:

(a)   Any person on whom an information, special information or enforcement notice has been served may appeal against it.

On such an appeal the Tribunal may review any question of fact on which the service of the notice was based. The Tribunal must dismiss the appeal unless it considers that one of the following two factors is true:

(i)   that the notice against which the appeal is brought does not accord with some legal provision, or

(ii)   that the Commissioner ought to have exercised her discretion (if any) differently.

If either factor is made out by the appellant then the Tribunal must allow the appeal or substitute the notice with any other notice which the Commissioner could have served.

(b)   A person who has been served with an enforcement notice may appeal against the refusal of an application under s. 41(2) for cancellation or variation of the notice.

Section 41(2) allows an application to the Commissioner for cancellation or variation of an enforcement notice (due to change of circumstances) where the time limit for an appeal against the notice has expired. Notwithstanding the expiry of the right to appeal against the notice itself, this provision allows an appeal against the decision of the Commissioner not to grant such variation or cancellation.

The Tribunal may cancel or vary the notice due to a change of circumstances where it feels it appropriate to do so.

(c)   A person who has been served with an information, special information or enforcement notice containing a statement of urgency for the purposes of imposing a shorter than normal time limit for compliance may appeal against the Commissioner's decision to include such a statement in the notice.

The Tribunal may abolish the effect of the statement.

(d)   A person who has been served with an information, special information or enforcement notice containing a statement of urgency for the purposes of imposing a shorter than normal time limit for compliance may appeal against the effect of the inclusion of the statement in respect of any part of the notice.

The Tribunal may direct that the inclusion of the statement shall not have effect in relation to any part of the notice.

(e)   A data controller may appeal against a determination under s. 45 that personal data are not being processed only for the special purposes or with a view to publication by any person of any journalistic, literary or artistic material which has not previously been published by the data controller.

The Tribunal may cancel the determination of the Commissioner.

Appeals from any decision of the Tribunal are available to either party and will be heard by the High Court of Justice (or the Court of Session where the appellant's address is in Scotland; the High Court of Justice of Northern Ireland where the appellant's address is in Northern Ireland).

Chapter 7
Criminal Offences

INTRODUCTION

The Data Protection Act 1998 creates a number of criminal offences which are contained in various parts of the Act. This chapter examines each of the offences in turn. Some have been dealt with in the text of chapters 2, 3, 4 and 6 where they have been relevant to the material contained in those chapters. Other offences are of a more general nature and will be dealt with here for the first time.

Criminal proceedings cannot be instituted except by the Commissioner or by or with the consent of the Director of Public Prosecutions (in Northern Ireland the Director of Public Prosecutions for Northern Ireland).

All offences contained in the Act are punishable only with a fine — imprisonment is not a possibility for contraventions of the Act. The offence contained in sch. 9, para. 12, is a summary-only offence punishable with a fine not exceeding level 5 on the standard scale. All other offences in the Act are either-way offences which may be tried in a magistrates' court or by jury in the Crown Court. The maximum fine on summary conviction is £5,000. In the Crown Court there is no maximum limit.

In the case of certain of the offences the court has power to order the forfeiture, destruction or erasure of a document, computer disk or other material used in connection with the processing of personal data. Where the owner of such a document, computer disk or other material is not the offender that person must be given the opportunity of making representations before the making of such an order for forfeiture, destruction or erasure.

UNLAWFUL OBTAINING OR DISCLOSURE OF PERSONAL DATA

By virtue of s. 55(1) a person must not knowingly or recklessly, without the consent of the data controller:

(a) obtain or disclose personal data or the information contained in personal data, or

(b) procure the disclosure to another person of the information contained in personal data.

For these purposes only, the definition of personal data does not include any personal data which are exempt on national security grounds (s. 55(8)).

Section 55(3) makes the contravention of s. 55(1) a criminal offence. A defence is available to any person charged with such an offence who shows:

(a)   that the obtaining, disclosing or procuring was necessary for the purpose of preventing or detecting crime, or was required or authorised by or under any enactment, by any rule of law or by the order of a court,

(b)   that the actions said to constitute the offence were taken in the reasonable belief of having in law the right to obtain or disclose the data or information or, as the case may be, to procure the disclosure of the information to the other person,

(c)   that the actions said to constitute the offence were taken in the reasonable belief that the consent of the data controller would have been given if the data controller had known of the obtaining, disclosing or procuring and the circumstances of it, or

(d)   that in the particular circumstances the obtaining, disclosing or procuring was justified as being in the public interest.

The creation of this offence deals with some of the problems created by the unsuccessful prosecution in *R v Brown* [1996] 2 WLR 203. In that case a police officer, in an attempt to assist a friend who ran a debt collection agency (Capital Investigations Ltd.), asked a colleague to call to a computer screen certain information held on the police national computer database. There was no evidence that the personal data revealed by the search was ever communicated by the officer to Capital Investigations or used by him in any other way. The officer was charged with the 1984 Act offence of using personal data for a purpose other than that described in the register. The police registration with the Registrar anticipated use of data for police purposes and did not cover the suspected activities of the officer in question.

The key to the prosecution lay in the word 'use' as it appeared in the 1984 Act. If the officer could be said to be using data then he was guilty. The defence case was that the officer was not using data, as he had merely read information appearing on a computer screen. He was found guilty by a jury but the conviction was overturned on appeal. The House of Lords held that 'use' was to be given its ordinary meaning and that the concept of use did not extend to mere retrieval of information from a database.

Section 55 of the Act makes it an offence to 'obtain' or 'disclose' information contained in personal data (or procure the disclosure to another person of the information contained in personal data). A person who acted today as Mr Brown had done would be guilty of this offence.

SELLING AND OFFERING TO SELL PERSONAL DATA

Section 55(4) creates an offence where a person sells personal data having obtained them in contravention of s. 55(1), which is discussed above.

Section 55(5) creates an offence which will be committed where a person offers to sell personal data and:

(a)   the person has obtained the data in contravention of s. 55(1), or

(b)   the person subsequently obtains the data in contravention of s. 55(1).

Subsections (4) and (5) of s. 55 cover the situations of both sale and offering for sale. A person may be guilty of offering for sale even where, at the point of offer, there has been no obtaining in contravention of s. 55(1) — the later obtaining of personal data in contravention of that subsection will outlaw the earlier offer.

The distinction between an offer and an invitation to treat is purely academic in relation to advertisements: by virtue of s. 55(6) all indications of the availability for sale of personal data which are contained in advertisements are to be treated as offers for sale for the purpose of this offence.

REQUIRING THE SUPPLY OF A RELEVANT RECORD

By virtue of s. 56(1) a person must not require another person (or a third party) to supply him with a relevant record (see definition below) or to produce a relevant record to him in connection with:

(a)   the recruitment of that other person as an employee,
(b)   the continued employment of that other person, or
(c)   any contract for the provision of services to him by that other person.

Section 56(2) provides that a person who is concerned with the provision of goods, facilities or services to the public must not, as a condition of such provision, require that other person or a third party to supply him with a relevant record or to produce a relevant record to him.

Section 56(5) makes the contravention of s. 56(1) or (2) a criminal offence. However, it will be a defence for a person charged with either offence to show that:

(a)   the imposition of the requirement was required or authorised by or under any enactment, by any rule of law or by the order of a court, or
(b)   in the particular circumstances the imposition of the requirement was justified as being in the public interest.

Subsection (4) of section 56 makes it clear that the imposition of a requirement is not to be regarded as being justified as being in the public interest merely on the ground that it would assist in the prevention or detection of crime, and contains a cross-reference to part V of the Police Act 1997.

'Relevant record' is defined, somewhat confusingly, by reference to a table (reproduced below) which consists of two columns. The left-hand column lists various data controllers, and the right-hand column, various types of relevant subject matter. A 'relevant record' is any record which:

(a)   has been or is to be obtained by a data subject from any data controller specified in the first column of the table in exercise of the subject access provisions in s. 7, and
(b)   contains information relating to any matter specified in relation to that data controller in the second column,

and includes a copy of such a record or a part of such a record.

TABLE

Data controller	Subject-matter
1. Any of the following persons— (a) a chief officer of police of a police force in England and Wales, (b) a chief constable of a police force in Scotland, (c) the Chief Constable of the Royal Ulster Constabulary, (d) the Director General of the National Criminal Intelligence Service, (e) the Director General of the National Crime Squad,	(a) Convictions. (b) Cautions.
2. The Secretary of State.	(a) Convictions. (b) Cautions. (c) His functions under section 53 of the Children and Young Persons Act 1933, section 205(2) or 208 of the Criminal Procedure (Scotland) Act 1995 or section 73 of the Children and Young Persons Act (Northern Ireland) 1968 in relation to any person sentenced to detention. (d) His functions under the Prison Act 1952, the Prisons (Scotland) Act 1989 or the Prison Act (Northern Ireland) 1953 in relation to any person imprisoned or detained. (e) His functions under the Social Security Contributions and Benefits Act 1992, the Social Security Administration Act 1992 or the Jobseekers Act 1995. (f) His functions under Part V of the Police Act 1997.
3. The Department of Health and Social Services for Northern Ireland.	Its functions under the Social Security Contributions and Benefits (Northern Ireland) Act 1992, the Social Security Administration (Northern Ireland) Act 1992 or the Jobseekers (Northern Ireland) Order 1995.

The table may be amended by the Secretary of State by order.

DISCLOSING THE COMMISSIONER'S INFORMATION

Section 59(1) contains a prohibition on the disclosing of certain information which has been provided to the office of the Commissioner. It is an offence knowingly or recklessly to disclose such information (s. 59(3)). The prohibition exists in relation to the following persons only:

(a)   the Commissioner,
(b)   a member of the Commissioner's staff,
(c)   an agent of the Commissioner.

The information which cannot be disclosed (unless the disclosure is made with lawful authority — see below) is that which:

(a)   has been obtained by, or furnished to, the Commissioner under or for the purposes of the Act,
(b)   relates to an identified or identifiable individual or business, and
(c)   is not at the time of the disclosure, and has not previously been, available to the public from other sources.

A disclosure is made with lawful authority only if one or more of the following apply:

(a)   the disclosure is made with the consent of the individual or of the person for the time being carrying on the business,
(b)   the information was provided for the purpose of its being made available to the public (in whatever manner) under any provision of the Act,
(c)   the disclosure is made for the purposes of, and is necessary for, the discharge of any function under the Act or any Community obligation,
(d)   the disclosure is made for the purposes of any proceedings, whether criminal or civil and whether arising under, or by virtue of, this Act or otherwise, or
(e)   having regard to the rights and freedoms or legitimate interests of any person, the disclosure is necessary in the public interest.

OBSTRUCTING OR FAILING TO ASSIST IN THE EXECUTION OF A WARRANT

Schedule 9 contains provisions allowing the application for a warrant to enter and inspect premises where there is a suspicion of contravention of the data protection principles or of a criminal offence having been committed under the Act. Paragraph 12 of that schedule makes it a criminal offence:

(a)   to intentionally obstruct a person in the execution of such a warrant, or
(b)   to fail without reasonable cause to give any person executing such a warrant such assistance as he or she may reasonably require for the execution of the warrant.

The offence is summary only and punishable only by a fine not exceeding level 5 on the standard scale.

PROCESSING WITHOUT A REGISTER ENTRY

Section 21(1) makes it a criminal offence to process personal data where all of the following apply:

(a)   an entry in the register maintained by the Commissioner has not been made,
(b)   the notification regulations (if any) relating to deemed registration do not apply,
(c)   notification regulations (if any) giving authority to certain specified types of processing without the need for notification do not apply, and
(d)   it is not the case that the sole purpose of the processing is the maintenance of a public register.

Manual records (and accessible records), even if they fall within the definition of data, are not subject to notification to the Commissioner and therefore processing them will not be a criminal offence under this provision (see chapter 4, 'Prohibition on processing').

FAILING TO NOTIFY CHANGES

Under s. 21(1) a data controller is under a duty to inform the Commissioner of any change in-

(a)   the registrable particulars, or
(b)   the measures taken to comply with the seventh principle.

What will and will not constitute a change for these purposes is to be set out in the notification regulations.

By virtue of s. 21(2), failure to notify the Commissioner of these changes constitutes the commission of a criminal offence. It is a defence to show that the defendant exercised all due diligence to comply with the duty.

CARRYING ON ASSESSABLE PROCESSING

Under s. 22(6) it is a criminal offence to carry on assessable processing (see chapter 4, 'Assessable processing') after notification to the Commissioner unless either:

(a)   the relevant period of 28 days (or longer if extended) has elapsed, or
(b)   before the end of the period in (a) the data controller has received a notice from the Commissioner stating the extent to which the Commissioner is of the opinion that the processing is likely or unlikely to comply with the provisions of the Act.

FAILING TO MAKE CERTAIN PARTICULARS AVAILABLE

Section 24 imposes a duty on a data controller who chooses not to register with the Commissioner where notification is not compulsory because:

(a)   the only personal data being processed are manual data recorded as part of a relevant filing system (and the processing is not assessable processing); or

(b)   the only personal data being processed are part of an accessible record (and the processing is not assessable processing); or

(c)   notification regulations provide that processing of that description does not require notification.

The duty under s. 24 is that the data controller must, within 21 days of receiving a written request from any person, make the relevant particulars available in writing to that person free of charge. The relevant particulars are items (a) to (f) of the registrable particulars listed in s. 16(1). Thus lack of notification and hence lack of registration does not mean that a data controller will not be required to make the appropriate disclosure to a data subject.

The Secretary of State may provide exemptions from the operation of s. 24 in the notification regulations.

It is a criminal offence to fail to comply with this duty of disclosure (s. 24(4)). It is a defence to show that the defendant exercised all due diligence to comply. Thus an accidental failure to set out the relevant particulars fully should escape conviction.

FAILING TO COMPLY WITH A NOTICE

By virtue of s. 47(1) it is an offence to fail to comply with an enforcement, an information or a special information notice (see chapter 6). It is a defence to show that the defendant exercised all due diligence to comply with the notice.

MAKING A FALSE STATEMENT IN RESPONSE TO A NOTICE

Under s. 47(2) it is an offence to make a false statement, knowingly or recklessly, in response to an information or special information notice (see chapter 6).

LIABILITY OF CORPORATE OFFICERS

Under s. 61(1) a director, manager, secretary or other similar officer of a corporate body may be liable to be punished for the same offence as that which has been proved against the corporate body by whom they are employed. In order to be found guilty of the offence the director etc. must be involved in the offence committed by the corporate body by virtue of some connivance or neglect. Similar rules exist in relation to a Scottish partnership (s. 61(3)).

A charge under s. 61(1) may be brought against a person who is a member of a corporate body where that body is managed by its members.

IMMUNITY FROM PROSECUTION

Although the Crown is subject to the provisions of the Data Protection Act 1998 in the same way as other persons, s. 63(5) provides that neither a government department nor a person who acts on behalf of the Royal Household, the Duchy of Lancaster or the Duchy of Cornwall in respect of certain types of data (see s. 63(3)) can be prosecuted for any offences contained in the Act.

Chapter 8
Transitional Provisions

INTRODUCTION

The operation of the Data Protection Act 1998 is complicated by the fact that its provisions come into force at various times. Certain sections came into force on 16 July 1998, the date of the passing of the statute. The bulk will enter into force in 1999. However, certain provisions are modified for certain durations. The two most important dates for these purposes are 24 October 2001 and 24 October 2007. This chapter sets out the reliefs and other provisions in sch. 14 which provide for the transition from the regime of the 1984 Act to that of the 1998 Act. Schedule 16, yet to be brought into force at the time of writing, repeals the 1984 Act in its entirety.

The transitional rights in s. 12A are considered in chapter 2, 'Transitional rights'. Transitional exemptions are the subject of part 2 of chapter 5.

In this chapter 'the old principles' means the data protection principles contained in the 1984 Act, and 'the new principles' those in the 1998 Act.

EFFECT OF 1984 ACT REGISTRATION

An application for registration under part II of the 1984 Act which is received by the Commissioner before the commencement of the notification provisions of the 1998 Act will be dealt with under the provisions of the old Act.

Under sch. 14, para. 2, a data controller may treat his 1984 Act registration (and deemed registration by virtue of s. 7(6) of the 1984 Act) as continuing for the purposes of the new Act until the earlier of the following two periods:

(a)   the date on which his entry in the register would have fallen to be removed under the old Act,

(b)   24 October 2001.

A data controller may therefore choose not to notify the Commissioner of any processing until the expiry of that period. The data controller will not be subject to the prohibition on processing in s. 17(1) by so doing. It is open to any data controller who could benefit by virtue of these provisions to register voluntarily under s. 18(1). Such registration will terminate the exemption in the above provisions.

The benefit of these provisions will cease in respect of a data controller who is treated as being registered under the old Act by virtue of s. 7(6) of that Act and who receives a notification under s. 7(1) of the 1984 Act of the refusal of his application. The date of such cessation will be:

(a)   if no appeal is brought, the end of the period during which an appeal can be brought against the refusal, or
(b)   the date of the withdrawal or dismissal of the appeal.

RIGHTS OF DATA SUBJECTS

Where a request under the 1984 Act for access to personal data is received by a data controller before the repeal of that Act, the request must be complied with even where the old Act is repealed prior to actual compliance.

Compensation for damage or distress under the old Act due to inaccuracy (Data Protection Act 1984, s. 22), or for loss or unauthorised disclosure (s. 23), continues to be claimable after the repeal of the relevant sections where the damage or distress was suffered before the commencement of the repeals (Data Protection Act 1998, sch. 14, para. 4).

An application to the court for rectification or erasure under the Data Protection Act 1984, s. 24, will be unaffected by the 1984 Act's repeal where it was made before the repeal comes into force.

The Data Protection Act 1998, s. 14(3)(b), which allows the court to order a data controller to notify third parties of the rectification, blocking, erasure or destruction of personal data where it is satisfied that the data were inaccurate, does not apply where the rectification, blocking, erasure or destruction occurred before the commencement of s. 14.

ENFORCEMENT

Paragraphs 7 and 8 of sch. 14 to the Data Protection Act 1998 deal with the transitional position in respect of enforcement notices. Where an enforcement notice under s. 10 of the 1984 Act has effect immediately before the commencement of s. 40 of the 1998 Act (which deals with the service of enforcement notices) and there can be no appeal from that enforcement notice, the notice will have effect for the purposes of s. 41 (cancellation of enforcement notices) and s. 47 (provisions relating to the failure to comply with a notice) after the commencement as if it were an enforcement notice under s. 40. Where, upon the commencement of s. 40, there was still the possibility of appeal against a notice served before the commencement, the appeal (if any) will be determined under the old Act.

A transfer prohibition notice under s. 12 of the 1984 Act will have effect as if it were an enforcement notice under s. 40 after the commencement of that section. Any appeal against a transfer prohibition notice heard after the commencement of s. 40 will be dealt with under the provisions of the old Act.

Service of notices

The Commissioner may serve an enforcement notice under s. 40 on or after the day the section comes into force if she is satisfied that the conduct which amounted to contravention of the old principles also constitutes contravention of the new principles.

An enforcement notice cannot require a data controller to notify third parties of any rectification, blocking, erasure or destruction under s. 40(5)(b) where it occurred before the commencement of s. 40.

The Commissioner may serve an information notice under s. 43 on or after the day the section comes into force if she has reasonable grounds for suspecting that the conduct which amounted to contravention of the old principles also constitutes contravention of the new principles.

Self-incrimination

The exemptions in s. 43(8) and s. 44(9) from furnishing information in response to an information or special information notice where that would expose the person on whom the notice was served to criminal proceedings apply to any criminal offence except offences created by the old Act as well as the new. The reference, in s. 34(9) of the old Act to an offence under that Act includes a reference to an offence under the new Act.

Appendix 1

Sections 158 to 160 Consumer Credit Act 1974, as amended by the Data Protection Act 1998

158   Duty of Agency to disclose filed information
(1)   A credit reference agency, within the prescribed period after receiving:

(a)   a request in writing to that effect from any partnership or other unincorporated body of persons not consisting entirely of bodies corporate (the 'consumer') and
(b)   such particulars as the agency may reasonably require to enable them to identify the file, and
(c)   a fee of [£1],

shall give the consumer a copy of the file relating to him kept by the agency.
(2)   When giving a copy of the file under subsection (1), the agency shall also give the consumer a statement in the prescribed form of the consumer's rights under section 159.
(3)   If the agency does not keep a file relating to the consumer it shall give the consumer notice of that fact, but need not return any money paid.
(4)   If the agency contravenes any provision of this section it commits an offence.
(5)   In this Act 'file', in relation to an individual, means all the information about him kept by a credit reference agency, regardless of how the information is stored and 'copy of the file', as respects information not in plain English, means a transcript reduced into plain English.

159   Correction of wrong information
(1)   Any individual (the 'objector') given—

(a)   information under section 7 of the Data Protection Act 1998 by a credit reference agency, or
(b)   information under section 158,

who considers that an entry in his file is incorrect, and that if it is not corrected he is likely to be prejudiced, may give notice to the agency requiring it either to remove the entry from the file or amend it.
(2)   Within 28 days after receiving a notice under subsection (1), the agency shall by notice inform the objector that it has—

(a)   removed the entry from the file, or

(b)   amended the entry, or

(c)   taken no action,

and if the notice states that the agency has amended the entry it shall include a copy of the file so far as it comprises the amended entry.

(3)   Within 28 days after receiving a notice under subsection (2) or, where no such notice was given, within 28 days after the expiry of the period mentioned in subsection (2), the objector may, unless he has been informed by the agency that it has removed the entry from his file, serve a further notice from the agency requiring it to add to the file the accompanying notice of correction (not exceeding 200 words) drawn up by the objector and include a copy of it when furnishing information included in or based on that entry.

(4)   Within 28 days after receiving a notice under subsection (3), the agency, unless it intends to apply to the relevant authority under subsection (5), shall by notice inform the objector that it has received the notice under subsection (3) and intends to comply with it.

(5)   If—

(a)   the objector has not received a notice under subsection (4) within the time required, or

(b)   it appears to the agency that it would be improper for it to publish a notice of correction because it is incorrect, or unjustly defames any person, or is frivolous or scandalous, or is for any other reason unsuitable,

the objector or, as the case may be, the agency may, in the prescribed manner and on payment of the specified fee, apply to the relevant authority, who make such order on the application as he thinks fit.

(6)   If a person to whom an order under this section is directed fails to comply with it within the period specified in the order he commits an offence.

(7)   The Data Protection Commissioner may vary or revoke any order made by him under this section.

(8)   In this section 'the relevant authority' means—

(a)   where the objector is a partnership or other unincorporated body of persons, the Director, and

(b)   in any other case the Data Protection Commissioner.

160   Alternative procedure for business consumers

(1)   The Director, on an application made by a credit reference agency, may direct that this section shall apply to the agency if he is satisfied—

(a)   that compliance with section 158 in the case of consumers who carry on a business would adversely affect the service provided to its customers by the agency, and

(b)   that, having regard to the methods employed by the agency and to any other relevant factors, it is probable that consumers carrying on a business would not be prejudiced by the making of the direction.

(2)   Where an agency to which this section applies receives a request, particulars and a fee under section 158(1) from a consumer who carries on a business, and section 158(3) does not apply, the agency, instead of complying with section 158, may elect to deal with the matter under the following subsections.

(3)   Instead of giving the consumer a copy of the file, the agency shall within the prescribed period give notice to the consumer that it is proceeding under this section, and by notice give the consumer such information included in or based on entries in the file as the Director may direct, together with a statement in the prescribed form of the consumer's rights under subsection (4) and (5).

(4)   If within 28 days after receiving the information given to the consumer under subsection (3), or such longer period as the Director may allow, the consumer—

(a)   gives notice to the Director that the consumer is dissatisfied with the information, and

(b)   satisfies the Director that the consumer has taken such steps in relation to the agency as may be reasonable with a view to removing the cause of the consumer's dissatisfaction, and

(c)   pays the Director the specified fee,

the Director may direct the agency to give the Director a copy of the file, and the Director may disclose to the consumer such of the information on the file as the Dirctor thinks fit.

(5)   Section 159 applies with any necessary modifications to information given to the consumer under this section as it applies to information given under section 158.

(6)   If an agency making an election under subsection (2) fails to comply with subsection (3) or (4) it commits an offence.

(7)   In this section 'consumer' has the same meaning as in section 158.

Data Protection Act 1998

CHAPTER 29

ARRANGEMENT OF SECTIONS

PART I
PRELIMINARY

PART II
RIGHTS OF DATA SUBJECTS AND OTHERS

PART III
NOTIFICATION BY DATA CONTROLLERS

PART IV
EXEMPTIONS

PART V
ENFORCEMENT

PART VI
MISCELLANEOUS AND GENERAL

Functions of Commissioner

Unlawful obtaining etc. of personal data

Data Protection Act 1998

1998 CHAPTER 29

An Act to make new provision for the regulation of the processing of information relating to individuals, including the obtaining, holding, use or disclosure of such information. [16th July 1998]

BE IT ENACTED by the Queen's most Excellent Majesty, by and with the advice and consent of the Lords Spiritual and Temporal, and Commons, in this present Parliament assembled, and by the authority of the same, as follows:

PART I

PRELIMINARY

1. Basic interpretative provisions

(1)   In this Act, unless the context otherwise requires—

'data' means information which—

   (a)   is being processed by means of equipment operating automatically in response to instructions given for that purpose,

   (b)   is recorded with the intention that it should be processed by means of such equipment,

   (c)   is recorded as part of a relevant filing system or with the intention that it should form part of a relevant filing system, or

   (d)   does not fall within paragraph (a), (b) or (c) but forms part of an accessible record as defined by section 68;

'data controller' means, subject to subsection (4), a person who (either alone or jointly or in common with other persons) determines the purposes for which and the manner in which any personal data are, or are to be, processed;

'data processor', in relation to personal data, means any person (other than an employee of the data controller) who processes the data on behalf of the data controller;

'data subject' means an individual who is the subject of personal data;

'personal data' means data which relate to a living individual who can be identified—

   (a)   from those data, or

(b)   from those data and other information which is in the possession of, or is likely to come into the possession of, the data controller,

and includes any expression of opinion about the individual and any indication of the intentions of the data controller or any other person in respect of the individual; 'processing', in relation to information or data, means obtaining, recording or holding the information or data or carrying out any operation or set of operations on the information or data, including—

     (a)   organisation, adaptation or alteration of the information or data,

     (b)   retrieval, consultation or use of the information or data,

     (c)   disclosure of the information or data by transmission, dissemination or otherwise making available, or

     (d)   alignment, combination, blocking, erasure or destruction of the information or data;

'relevant filing system' means any set of information relating to individuals to the extent that, although the information is not processed by means of equipment operating automatically in response to instructions given for that purpose, the set is structured, either by reference to individuals or by reference to criteria relating to individuals, in such a way that specific information relating to a particular individual is readily accessible.

(2)   In this Act, unless the context otherwise requires—

     (a)   'obtaining' or 'recording', in relation to personal data, includes obtaining or recording the information to be contained in the data, and

     (b)   'using' or 'disclosing', in relation to personal data, includes using or disclosing the information contained in the data.

(3)   In determining for the purposes of this Act whether any information is recorded with the intention—

     (a)   that it should be processed by means of equipment operating automatically in response to instructions given for that purpose, or

     (b)   that it should form part of a relevant filing system,

it is immaterial that it is intended to be so processed or to form part of such a system only after being transferred to a country or territory outside the European Economic Area.

(4)   Where personal data are processed only for purposes for which they are required by or under any enactment to be processed, the person on whom the obligation to process the data is imposed by or under that enactment is for the purposes of this Act the data controller.

2.   Sensitive personal data

In this Act 'sensitive personal data' means personal data consisting of information as to—

     (a)   the racial or ethnic origin of the data subject,

     (b)   his political opinions,

     (c)   his religious beliefs or other beliefs of a similar nature,

     (d)   whether he is a member of a trade union (within the meaning of the Trade Union and Labour Relations (Consolidation) Act 1992),

     (e)   his physical or mental health or condition,

     (f)   his sexual life,

     (g)   the commission or alleged commission by him of any offence, or

(h)   any proceedings for any offence committed or alleged to have been committed by him, the disposal of such proceedings or the sentence of any court in such proceedings.

3.   The special purposes

In this Act 'the special purposes' means any one or more of the following—

(a)   the purposes of journalism,

(b)   artistic purposes, and

(c)   literary purposes.

4.   The data protection principles

(1)   References in this Act to the data protection principles are to the principles set out in Part I of Schedule 1.

(2)   Those principles are to be interpreted in accordance with Part II of Schedule 1.

(3)   Schedule 2 (which applies to all personal data) and Schedule 3 (which applies only to sensitive personal data) set out conditions applying for the purposes of the first principle; and Schedule 4 sets out cases in which the eighth principle does not apply.

(4)   Subject to section 27(1), it shall be the duty of a data controller to comply with the data protection principles in relation to all personal data with respect to which he is the data controller.

5.   Application of Act

(1)   Except as otherwise provided by or under section 54, this Act applies to a data controller in respect of any data only if—

(a)   the data controller is established in the United Kingdom and the data are processed in the context of that establishment, or

(b)   the data controller is established neither in the United Kingdom nor in any other EEA State but uses equipment in the United Kingdom for processing the data otherwise than for the purposes of transit through the United Kingdom.

(2)   A data controller falling within subsection (1)(b) must nominate for the purposes of this Act a representative established in the United Kingdom.

(3)   For the purposes of subsections (1) and (2), each of the following is to be treated as established in the United Kingdom—

(a)   an individual who is ordinarily resident in the United Kingdom,

(b)   a body incorporated under the law of, or of any part of, the United Kingdom,

(c)   a partnership or other unincorporated association formed under the law of any part of the United Kingdom, and

(d)   any person who does not fall within paragraph (a), (b) or (c) but maintains in the United Kingdom—

(i)   an office, branch or agency through which he carries on any activity, or

(ii)   a regular practice;

and the reference to establishment in any other EEA State has a corresponding meaning.

6.   The Commissioner and the Tribunal

(1)   The office originally established by section 3(1)(a) of the Data Protection Act 1984 as the office of Data Protection Registrar shall continue to exist for the purposes

of this Act but shall be known as the office of Data Protection Commissioner; and in this Act the Data Protection Commissioner is referred to as 'the Commissioner'.

(2)   The Commissioner shall be appointed by Her Majesty by Letters Patent.

(3)   For the purposes of this Act there shall continue to be a Data Protection Tribunal (in this Act referred to as 'the Tribunal').

(4)   The Tribunal shall consist of—

(a)   a chairman appointed by the Lord Chancellor after consultation with the Lord Advocate,

(b)   such number of deputy chairmen so appointed as the Lord Chancellor may determine, and

(c) such number of other members appointed by the Secretary of State as he may determine.

(5)   The members of the Tribunal appointed under subsection (4)(a) and (b) shall be—

(a)   persons who have a 7 year general qualification, within the meaning of section 71 of the Courts and Legal Services Act 1990,

(b)   advocates or solicitors in Scotland of at least 7 years' standing, or

(c)   members of the bar of Northern Ireland or solicitors of the Supreme Court of Northern Ireland of at least 7 years' standing.

(6)   The members of the Tribunal appointed under subsection (4)(c) shall be—

(a)   persons to represent the interests of data subjects, and

(b)   persons to represent the interests of data controllers.

(7)   Schedule 5 has effect in relation to the Commissioner and the Tribunal.

PART II
RIGHTS OF DATA SUBJECTS AND OTHERS

7.   Right of access to personal data

(1)   Subject to the following provisions of this section and to sections 8 and 9, an individual is entitled—

(a)   to be informed by any data controller whether personal data of which that individual is the data subject are being processed by or on behalf of that data controller,

(b)   if that is the case, to be given by the data controller a description of—

(i)   the personal data of which that individual is the data subject,

(ii)   the purposes for which they are being or are to be processed, and

(iii)   the recipients or classes of recipients to whom they are or may be disclosed,

(c)   to have communicated to him in an intelligible form—

(i)   the information constituting any personal data of which that individual is the data subject, and

(ii)   any information available to the data controller as to the source of those data, and

(d)   where the processing by automatic means of personal data of which that individual is the data subject for the purpose of evaluating matters relating to him such as, for example, his performance at work, his creditworthiness, his reliability or his conduct, has constituted or is likely to constitute the sole basis for any decision significantly affecting him, to be informed by the data controller of the logic involved in that decision-taking.

(2)   A data controller is not obliged to supply any information under subsection (1) unless he has received—

(a)   a request in writing, and

(b)   except in prescribed cases, such fee (not exceeding the prescribed maximum) as he may require.

(3)   A data controller is not obliged to comply with a request under this section unless he is supplied with such information as he may reasonably require in order to satisfy himself as to the identity of the person making the request and to locate the information which that person seeks.

(4)   Where a data controller cannot comply with the request without disclosing information relating to another individual who can be identified from that information, he is not obliged to comply with the request unless—

(a)   the other individual has consented to the disclosure of the information to the person making the request, or

(b)   it is reasonable in all the circumstances to comply with the request without the consent of the other individual.

(5)   In subsection (4) the reference to information relating to another individual includes a reference to information identifying that individual as the source of the information sought by the request; and that subsection is not to be construed as excusing a data controller from communicating so much of the information sought by the request as can be communicated without disclosing the identity of the other individual concerned, whether by the omission of names or other identifying particulars or otherwise.

(6)   In determining for the purposes of subsection (4)(b) whether it is reasonable in all the circumstances to comply with the request without the consent of the other individual concerned, regard shall be had, in particular, to—

(a)   any duty of confidentiality owed to the other individual,

(b)   any steps taken by the data controller with a view to seeking the consent of the other individual,

(c)   whether the other individual is capable of giving consent, and

(d)   any express refusal of consent by the other individual.

(7)   An individual making a request under this section may, in such cases as may be prescribed, specify that his request is limited to personal data of any prescribed description.

(8)   Subject to subsection (4), a data controller shall comply with a request under this section promptly and in any event before the end of the prescribed period beginning with the relevant day.

(9)   If a court is satisfied on the application of any person who has made a request under the foregoing provisions of this section that the data controller in question has failed to comply with the request in contravention of those provisions, the court may order him to comply with the request.

(10)   In this section—

'prescribed' means prescribed by the Secretary of State by regulations;

'the prescribed maximum' means such amount as may be prescribed;

'the prescribed period' means forty days or such other period as may be prescribed;

'the relevant day', in relation to a request under this section, means the day on which the data controller receives the request or, if later, the first day on which the data controller has both the required fee and the information referred to in subsection (3).

(11)   Different amounts or periods may be prescribed under this section in relation to different cases.

8.   Provisions supplementary to section 7

(1)   The Secretary of State may by regulations provide that, in such cases as may be prescribed, a request for information under any provision of subsection (1) of section 7 is to be treated as extending also to information under other provisions of that subsection.

(2)   The obligation imposed by section 7(1)(c)(i) must be complied with by supplying the data subject with a copy of the information in permanent form unless—

(a)   the supply of such a copy is not possible or would involve disproportionate effort, or

(b)   the data subject agrees otherwise;

and where any of the information referred to in section 7(1)(c)(i) is expressed in terms which are not intelligible without explanation the copy must be accompanied by an explanation of those terms.

(3)   Where a data controller has previously complied with a request made under section 7 by an individual, the data controller is not obliged to comply with a subsequent identical or similar request under that section by that individual unless a reasonable interval has elapsed between compliance with the previous request and the making of the current request.

(4)   In determining for the purposes of subsection (3) whether requests under section 7 are made at reasonable intervals, regard shall be had to the nature of the data, the purpose for which the data are processed and the frequency with which the data are altered.

(5)   Section 7(1)(d) is not to be regarded as requiring the provision of information as to the logic involved in any decision-taking if, and to the extent that, the information constitutes a trade secret.

(6)   The information to be supplied pursuant to a request under section 7 must be supplied by reference to the data in question at the time when the request is received, except that it may take account of any amendment or deletion made between that time and the time when the information is supplied, being an amendment or deletion that would have been made regardless of the receipt of the request.

(7)   For the purposes of section 7(4) and (5) another individual can be identified from the information being disclosed if he can be identified from that information, or from that and any other information which, in the reasonable belief of the data controller, is likely to be in, or to come into, the possession of the data subject making the request.

9.   Application of section 7 where data controller is credit reference agency

(1)   Where the data controller is a credit reference agency, section 7 has effect subject to the provisions of this section.

(2)   An individual making a request under section 7 may limit his request to personal data relevant to his financial standing, and shall be taken to have so limited his request unless the request shows a contrary intention.

(3)   Where the data controller receives a request under section 7 in a case where personal data of which the individual making the request is the data subject are being processed by or on behalf of the data controller, the obligation to supply information under that section includes an obligation to give the individual making the request a

statement, in such form as may be prescribed by the Secretary of State by regulations, of the individual's rights—

    (a)   under section 159 of the Consumer Credit Act 1974 , and

    (b)   to the extent required by the prescribed form, under this Act.

10.   Right to prevent processing likely to cause damage or distress

(1)   Subject to subsection (2), an individual is entitled at any time by notice in writing to a data controller to require the data controller at the end of such period as is reasonable in the circumstances to cease, or not to begin, processing, or processing for a specified purpose or in a specified manner, any personal data in respect of which he is the data subject, on the ground that, for specified reasons—

    (a)   the processing of those data or their processing for that purpose or in that manner is causing or is likely to cause substantial damage or substantial distress to him or to another, and

    (b)   that damage or distress is or would be unwarranted.

(2)   Subsection (1) does not apply—

    (a)   in a case where any of the conditions in paragraphs 1 to 4 of Schedule 2 is met, or

    (b)   in such other cases as may be prescribed by the Secretary of State by order.

(3)   The data controller must within twenty-one days of receiving a notice under subsection (1) ('the data subject notice') give the individual who gave it a written notice—

    (a)   stating that he has complied or intends to comply with the data subject notice, or

    (b)   stating his reasons for regarding the data subject notice as to any extent unjustified and the extent (if any) to which he has complied or intends to comply with it.

(4)   If a court is satisfied, on the application of any person who has given a notice under subsection (1) which appears to the court to be justified (or to be justified to any extent), that the data controller in question has failed to comply with the notice, the court may order him to take such steps for complying with the notice (or for complying with it to that extent) as the court thinks fit.

(5)   The failure by a data subject to exercise the right conferred by subsection (1) or section 11 (1) does not affect any other right conferred on him by this Part.

11.   Right to prevent processing for purposes of direct marketing

(1)   An individual is entitled at any time by notice in writing to a data controller to require the data controller at the end of such period as is reasonable in the circumstances to cease, or not to begin, processing for the purposes of direct marketing personal data in respect of which he is the data subject.

(2)   If the court is satisfied, on the application of any person who has given a notice under subsection (1), that the data controller has failed to comply with the notice, the court may order him to take such steps for complying with the notice as the court thinks fit.

(3)   In this section 'direct marketing' means the communication (by whatever means) of any advertising or marketing material which is directed to particular individuals.

12.   Rights in relation to automated decision-taking

(1)   An individual is entitled at any time, by notice in writing to any data controller, to require the data controller to ensure that no decision taken by or on behalf of the data controller which significantly affects that individual is based solely on the processing by automatic means of personal data in respect of which that individual is the data subject for the purpose of evaluating matters relating to him such as, for example, his performance at work, his creditworthiness, his reliability or his conduct.

(2)   Where, in a case where no notice under subsection (1) has effect, a decision which significantly affects an individual is based solely on such processing as is mentioned in subsection (1)—

(a)   the data controller must as soon as reasonably practicable notify the individual that the decision was taken on that basis, and

(b)   the individual is entitled, within twenty-one days of receiving that notification from the data controller, by notice in writing to require the data controller to reconsider the decision or to take a new decision otherwise than on that basis.

(3)   The data controller must, within twenty-one days of receiving a notice under subsection (2)(b) ('the data subject notice') give the individual a written notice specifying the steps that he intends to take to comply with the data subject notice.

(4)   A notice under subsection (1) does not have effect in relation to an exempt decision; and nothing in subsection (2) applies to an exempt decision.

(5)   In subsection (4) 'exempt decision' means any decision—

(a)   in respect of which the condition in subsection (6) and the condition in subsection (7) are met, or

(b)   which is made in such other circumstances as may be prescribed by the Secretary of State by order.

(6)   The condition in this subsection is that the decision—

(a)   is taken in the course of steps taken—

(i)   for the purpose of considering whether to enter into a contract with the data subject,

(ii)   with a view to entering into such a contract, or

(iii)   in the course of performing such a contract, or

(b)   is authorised or required by or under any enactment.

(7)   The condition in this subsection is that either—

(a)   the effect of the decision is to grant a request of the data subject, or

(b)   steps have been taken to safeguard the legitimate interests of the data subject (for example, by allowing him to make representations).

(8)   If a court is satisfied on the application of a data subject that a person taking a decision in respect of him ('the responsible person') has failed to comply with subsection (1) or (2)(b), the court may order the responsible person to reconsider the decision, or to take a new decision which is not based solely on such processing as is mentioned in subsection (1).

(9)   An order under subsection (8) shall not affect the rights of any person other than the data subject and the responsible person.

13.   Compensation for failure to comply with certain requirements

(1)   An individual who suffers damage by reason of any contravention by a data controller of any of the requirements of this Act is entitled to compensation from the data controller for that damage.

(2)   An individual who suffers distress by reason of any contravention by a data controller of any of the requirements of this Act is entitled to compensation from the data controller for that distress if—

(a)   the individual also suffers damage by reason of the contravention, or

(b)   the contravention relates to the processing of personal data for the special purposes.

(3)   In proceedings brought against a person by virtue of this section it is a defence to prove that he had taken such care as in all the circumstances was reasonably required to comply with the requirement concerned.

14.   Rectification, blocking, erasure and destruction

(1)   If a court is satisfied on the application of a data subject that personal data of which the applicant is the subject are inaccurate, the court may order the data controller to rectify, block, erase or destroy those data and any other personal data in respect of which he is the data controller and which contain an expression of opinion which appears to the court to be based on the inaccurate data.

(2)   Subsection (1) applies whether or not the data accurately record information received or obtained by the data controller from the data subject or a third party but where the data accurately record such information, then—

(a)   if the requirements mentioned in paragraph 7 of Part II of Schedule 1 have been complied with, the court may, instead of making an order under subsection (1), make an order requiring the data to be supplemented by such statement of the true facts relating to the matters dealt with by the data as the court may approve, and

(b)   if all or any of those requirements have not been complied with, the court may, instead of making an order under that subsection, make such order as it thinks fit for securing compliance with those requirements with or without a further order requiring the data to be supplemented by such a statement as is mentioned in paragraph (a).

(3)   Where the court—

(a)   makes an order under subsection (1), or

(b)   is satisfied on the application of a data subject that personal data of which he was the data subject and which have been rectified, blocked, erased or destroyed were inaccurate,

it may, where it considers it reasonably practicable, order the data controller to notify third parties to whom the data have been disclosed of the rectification, blocking, erasure or destruction.

(4)   If a court is satisfied on the application of a data subject—

(a)   that he has suffered damage by reason of any contravention by a data controller of any of the requirements of this Act in respect of any personal data, in circumstances entitling him to compensation under section 13, and

(b)   that there is a substantial risk of further contravention in respect of those data in such circumstances,

the court may order the rectification, blocking, erasure or destruction of any of those data.

(5)   Where the court makes an order under subsection (4) it may, where it considers it reasonably practicable, order the data controller to notify third parties to whom the data have been disclosed of the rectification, blocking, erasure or destruction.

(6)   In determining whether it is reasonably practicable to require such notification as is mentioned in subsection (3) or (5) the court shall have regard, in particular, to the number of persons who would have to be notified.

15.   Jurisdiction and procedure

(1)   The jurisdiction conferred by sections 7 to 14 is exercisable by the High Court or a county court or, in Scotland, by the Court of Session or the sheriff.

(2)   For the purpose of determining any question whether an applicant under subsection (9) of section 7 is entitled to the information which he seeks (including any question whether any relevant data are exempt from that section by virtue of Part IV) a court may require the information constituting any data processed by or on behalf of the data controller and any information as to the logic involved in any decision-taking as mentioned in section 7(1)(d) to be made available for its own inspection but shall not, pending the determination of that question in the applicant's favour, require the information sought by the applicant to be disclosed to him or his representatives whether by discovery (or, in Scotland, recovery) or otherwise.

PART III

NOTIFICATION BY DATA CONTROLLERS

16.   Preliminary

(1)   In this Part 'the registrable particulars', in relation to a data controller, means—

(a)   his name and address,

(b)   if he has nominated a representative for the purposes of this Act, the name and address of the representative,

(c)   a description of the personal data being or to be processed by or on behalf of the data controller and of the category or categories of data subject to which they relate,

(d)   a description of the purpose or purposes for which the data are being or are to be processed,

(e)   a description of any recipient or recipients to whom the data controller intends or may wish to disclose the data,

(f)   the names, or a description of, any countries or territories outside the European Economic Area to which the data controller directly or indirectly transfers, or intends or may wish directly or indirectly to transfer, the data, and

(g)   in any case where—

(i)   personal data are being, or are intended to be, processed in circumstances in which the prohibition in subsection (1) of section 17 is excluded by subsection (2) or (3) of that section, and

(ii)   the notification does not extend to those data,

a statement of that fact.

(2)   In this Part—

'fees regulations' means regulations made by the Secretary of State under section 18(5) or 19(4) or (7);

'notification regulations' means regulations made by the Secretary of State under the other provisions of this Part;

'prescribed', except where used in relation to fees regulations, means prescribed by notification regulations.

(3)   For the purposes of this Part, so far as it relates to the addresses of data controllers—

(a)   the address of a registered company is that of its registered office, and

(b)   the address of a person (other than a registered company) carrying on a business is that of his principal place of business in the United Kingdom.

17.   Prohibition on processing without registration

(1)   Subject to the following provisions of this section, personal data must not be processed unless an entry in respect of the data controller is included in the register maintained by the Commissioner under section 19 (or is treated by notification regulations made by virtue of section 19(3) as being so included).

(2)   Except where the processing is assessable processing for the purposes of section 22, subsection (1) does not apply in relation to personal data consisting of information which falls neither within paragraph (a) of the definition of 'data' in section 1(1) nor within paragraph (b) of that definition.

(3)   If it appears to the Secretary of State that processing of a particular description is unlikely to prejudice the rights and freedoms of data subjects, notification regulations may provide that, in such cases as may be prescribed, subsection (1) is not to apply in relation to processing of that description.

(4)   Subsection (1) does not apply in relation to any processing whose sole purpose is the maintenance of a public register.

18.   Notification by data controllers

(1)   Any data controller who wishes to be included in the register maintained under section 19 shall give a notification to the Commissioner under this section.

(2)   A notification under this section must specify in accordance with notification regulations—

(a)   the registrable particulars, and

(b)   a general description of measures to be taken for the purpose of complying with the seventh data protection principle.

(3)   Notification regulations made by virtue of subsection (2) may provide for the determination by the Commissioner, in accordance with any requirements of the regulations, of the form in which the registrable particulars and the description mentioned in subsection (2)(b) are to be specified, including in particular the detail required for the purposes of section 16(1)(c), (d), (e) and (f) and subsection (2)(b).

(4)   Notification regulations may make provision as to the giving of notification—

(a)   by partnerships, or

(b)   in other cases where two or more persons are the data controllers in respect of any personal data.

(5)   The notification must be accompanied by such fee as may be prescribed by fees regulations.

(6)   Notification regulations may provide for any fee paid under subsection (5) or section 19(4) to be refunded in prescribed circumstances.

19.   Register of notifications

(1)   The Commissioner shall—

(a)   maintain a register of persons who have given notification under section 18, and

(b)   make an entry in the register in pursuance of each notification received by him under that section from a person in respect of whom no entry as data controller was for the time being included in the register.

(2)   Each entry in the register shall consist of—

(a)   the registrable particulars notified under section 18 or, as the case requires, those particulars as amended in pursuance of section 20(4), and

(b)   such other information as the Commissioner may be authorised or required by notification regulations to include in the register.

(3)   Notification regulations may make provision as to the time as from which any entry in respect of a data controller is to be treated for the purposes of section 17 as having been made in the register.

(4)   No entry shall be retained in the register for more than the relevant time except on payment of such fee as may be prescribed by fees regulations.

(5)   In subsection (4) 'the relevant time' means twelve months or such other period as may be prescribed by notification regulations; and different periods may be prescribed in relation to different cases.

(6)   The Commissioner—

(a)   shall provide facilities for making the information contained in the entries in the register available for inspection (in visible and legible form) by members of the public at all reasonable hours and free of charge, and

(b)   may provide such other facilities for making the information contained in those entries available to the public free of charge as he considers appropriate.

(7)   The Commissioner shall, on payment of such fee, if any, as may be prescribed by fees regulations, supply any member of the public with a duly certified copy in writing of the particulars contained in any entry made in the register.

20.   Duty to notify changes

(1)   For the purpose specified in subsection (2), notification regulations shall include provision imposing on every person in respect of whom an entry as a data controller is for the time being included in the register maintained under section 19 a duty to notify to the Commissioner, in such circumstances and at such time or times and in such form as may be prescribed, such matters relating to the registrable particulars and measures taken as mentioned in section 18(2)(b) as may be prescribed.

(2)   The purpose referred to in subsection (1) is that of ensuring, so far as practicable, that at any time—

(a)   the entries in the register maintained under section 19 contain current names and addresses and describe the current practice or intentions of the data controller with respect to the processing of personal data, and

(b)   the Commissioner is provided with a general description of measures currently being taken as mentioned in section 18(2)(b).

(3)   Subsection (3) of section 18 has effect in relation to notification regulations made by virtue of subsection (1) as it has effect in relation to notification regulations made by virtue of subsection (2) of that section.

(4)   On receiving any notification under notification regulations made by virtue of subsection (1), the Commissioner shall make such amendments of the relevant entry in the register maintained under section 19 as are necessary to take account of the notification.

21. Offences

(1)   If section 17(1) is contravened, the data controller is guilty of an offence.

(2)   Any person who fails to comply with the duty imposed by notification regulations made by virtue of section 20(1) is guilty of an offence.

(3)   It shall be a defence for a person charged with an offence under subsection (2) to show that he exercised all due diligence to comply with the duty.

22. Preliminary assessment by Commissioner

(1)   In this section 'assessable processing' means processing which is of a description specified in an order made by the Secretary of State as appearing to him to be particularly likely—

(a)   to cause substantial damage or substantial distress to data subjects, or

(b)   otherwise significantly to prejudice the rights and freedoms of data subjects.

(2)   On receiving notification from any data controller under section 18 or under notification regulations made by virtue of section 20 the Commissioner shall consider—

(a)   whether any of the processing to which the notification relates is assessable processing, and

(b)   if so, whether the assessable processing is likely to comply with the provisions of this Act.

(3)   Subject to subsection (4), the Commissioner shall, within the period of twenty-eight days beginning with the day on which he receives a notification which relates to assessable processing, give a notice to the data controller stating the extent to which the Commissioner is of the opinion that the processing is likely or unlikely to comply with the provisions of this Act.

(4)   Before the end of the period referred to in subsection (3) the Commissioner may, by reason of special circumstances, extend that period on one occasion only by notice to the data controller by such further period not exceeding fourteen days as the Commissioner may specify in the notice.

(5)   No assessable processing in respect of which a notification has been given to the Commissioner as mentioned in subsection (2) shall be carried on unless either—

(a)   the period of twenty-eight days beginning with the day on which the notification is received by the Commissioner (or, in a case falling within subsection (4), that period as extended under that subsection) has elapsed, or

(b)   before the end of that period (or that period as so extended) the data controller has received a notice from the Commissioner under subsection (3) in respect of the processing.

(6)   Where subsection (5) is contravened, the data controller is guilty of an offence.

(7)   The Secretary of State may by order amend subsections (3), (4) and (5) by substituting for the number of days for the time being specified there a different number specified in the order.

23. Power to make provision for appointment of data protection supervisors

(1)   The Secretary of State may by order—

(a)   make provision under which a data controller may appoint a person to act as a data protection supervisor responsible in particular for monitoring in an independent manner the data controller's compliance with the provisions of this Act, and

(b)   provide that, in relation to any data controller who has appointed a data protection supervisor in accordance with the provisions of the order and who complies with such conditions as may be specified in the order, the provisions of this Part are to have effect subject to such exemptions or other modifications as may be specified in the order.

(2)   An order under this section may—

(a)   impose duties on data protection supervisors in relation to the Commissioner, and

(b)   confer functions on the Commissioner in relation to data protection supervisors.

24.   Duty of certain data controllers to make certain information available

(1)   Subject to subsection (3), where personal data are processed in a case where—

(a)   by virtue of subsection (2) or (3) of section 17, subsection (1) of that section does not apply to the processing, and

(b)   the data controller has not notified the relevant particulars in respect of that processing under section 18,

the data controller must, within twenty-one days of receiving a written request from any person, make the relevant particulars available to that person in writing free of charge.

(2)   In this section 'the relevant particulars' means the particulars referred to in paragraphs (a) to (f) of section 16(1).

(3)   This section has effect subject to any exemption conferred for the purposes of this section by notification regulations.

(4)   Any data controller who fails to comply with the duty imposed by subsection (1) is guilty of an offence.

(5)   It shall be a defence for a person charged with an offence under subsection (4) to show that he exercised all due diligence to comply with the duty.

25.   Functions of Commissioner in relation to making of notification regulations

(1)   As soon as practicable after the passing of this Act, the Commissioner shall submit to the Secretary of State proposals as to the provisions to be included in the first notification regulations.

(2)   The Commissioner shall keep under review the working of notification regulations and may from time to time submit to the Secretary of State proposals as to amendments to be made to the regulations.

(3)   The Secretary of State may from time to time require the Commissioner to consider any matter relating to notification regulations and to submit to him proposals as to amendments to be made to the regulations in connection with that matter.

(4)   Before making any notification regulations, the Secretary of State shall—

(a)   consider any proposals made to him by the Commissioner under subsection (1), (2) or (3), and

(b)   consult the Commissioner.

26.   Fees regulations

(1)   Fees regulations prescribing fees for the purposes of any provision of this Part may provide for different fees to be payable in different cases.

(2)   In making any fees regulations, the Secretary of State shall have regard to the desirability of securing that the fees payable to the Commissioner are sufficient to offset—

(a)   the expenses incurred by the Commissioner and the Tribunal in discharging their functions and any expenses of the Secretary of State in respect of the Commissioner or the Tribunal, and

(b)   to the extent that the Secretary of State considers appropriate—

(i)   any deficit previously incurred (whether before or after the passing of this Act) in respect of the expenses mentioned in paragraph (a), and

(ii)   expenses incurred or to be incurred by the Secretary of State in respect of the inclusion of any officers or staff of the Commissioner in any scheme under section 1 of the Superannuation Act 1972.

PART IV
EXEMPTIONS

27.   Preliminary

(1)   References in any of the data protection principles or any provision of Parts II and III to personal data or to the processing of personal data do not include references to data or processing which by virtue of this Part are exempt from that principle or other provision.

(2)   In this Part 'the subject information provisions' means—

(a)   the first data protection principle to the extent to which it requires compliance with paragraph 2 of Part II of Schedule 1, and

(b)   section 7.

(3)   In this Part 'the non-disclosure provisions' means the provisions specified in subsection (4) to the extent to which they are inconsistent with the disclosure in question.

(4)   The provisions referred to in subsection (3) are—

(a)   the first data protection principle, except to the extent to which it requires compliance with the conditions in Schedules 2 and 3,

(b)   the second, third, fourth and fifth data protection principles, and

(c)   sections 10 and 14(1) to (3).

(5)   Except as provided by this Part, the subject information provisions shall have effect notwithstanding any enactment or rule of law prohibiting or restricting the disclosure, or authorising the withholding, of information.

28.   National security

(1)   Personal data are exempt from any of the provisions of—

(a)   the data protection principles,

(b)   Parts II, III and V, and

(c)   section 55,

if the exemption from that provision is required for the purpose of safeguarding national security.

(2)   Subject to subsection (4), a certificate signed by a Minister of the Crown certifying that exemption from all or any of the provisions mentioned in subsection (1) is or at any time was required for the purpose there mentioned in respect of any personal data shall be conclusive evidence of that fact.

(3)   A certificate under subsection (2) may identify the personal data to which it applies by means of a general description and may be expressed to have prospective effect.

(4)   Any person directly affected by the issuing of a certificate under subsection (2) may appeal to the Tribunal against the certificate.

(5)   If on an appeal under subsection (4), the Tribunal finds that, applying the principles applied by the court on an application for judicial review, the Minister did not have reasonable grounds for issuing the certificate, the Tribunal may allow the appeal and quash the certificate.

(6)   Where in any proceedings under or by virtue of this Act it is claimed by a data controller that a certificate under subsection (2) which identifies the personal data to which it applies by means of a general description applies to any personal data, any other party to the proceedings may appeal to the Tribunal on the ground that the certificate does not apply to the personal data in question and, subject to any determination under subsection (7), the certificate shall be conclusively presumed so to apply.

(7)   On any appeal under subsection (6), the Tribunal may determine that the certificate does not so apply.

(8)   A document purporting to be a certificate under subsection (2) shall be received in evidence and deemed to be such a certificate unless the contrary is proved.

(9)   A document which purports to be certified by or on behalf of a Minister of the Crown as a true copy of a certificate issued by that Minister under subsection (2) shall in any legal proceedings be evidence (or, in Scotland, sufficient evidence) of that certificate.

(10)   The power conferred by subsection (2) on a Minister of the Crown shall not be exercisable except by a Minister who is a member of the Cabinet or by the Attorney General or the Lord Advocate.

(11)   No power conferred by any provision of Part V may be exercised in relation to personal data which by virtue of this section are exempt from that provision.

(12)   Schedule 6 shall have effect in relation to appeals under subsection (4) or (6) and the proceedings of the Tribunal in respect of any such appeal.

29.   Crime and taxation

(1)   Personal data processed for any of the following purposes—

    (a)   the prevention or detection of crime,

    (b)   the apprehension or prosecution of offenders, or

    (c)   the assessment or collection of any tax or duty or of any imposition of a similar nature,

are exempt from the first data protection principle (except to the extent to which it requires compliance with the conditions in Schedules 2 and 3) and section 7 in any case to the extent to which the application of those provisions to the data would be likely to prejudice any of the matters mentioned in this subsection.

(2)   Personal data which—

    (a)   are processed for the purpose of discharging statutory functions, and

    (b)   consist of information obtained for such a purpose from a person who had it in his possession for any of the purposes mentioned in subsection (1),

are exempt from the subject information provisions to the same extent as personal data processed for any of the purposes mentioned in that subsection.

(3)   Personal data are exempt from the non-disclosure provisions in any case in which—

    (a)   the disclosure is for any of the purposes mentioned in subsection (1), and

    (b)   the application of those provisions in relation to the disclosure would be likely to prejudice any of the matters mentioned in that subsection.

(4)   Personal data in respect of which the data controller is a relevant authority and which—

    (a)   consist of a classification applied to the data subject as part of a system of risk assessment which is operated by that authority for either of the following purposes—

        (i)   the assessment or collection of any tax or duty or any imposition of a similar nature, or

        (ii)   the prevention or detection of crime, or apprehension or prosecution of offenders, where the offence concerned involves any unlawful claim for any payment out of, or any unlawful application of, public funds, and

    (b)   are processed for either of those purposes,

are exempt from section 7 to the extent to which the exemption is required in the interests of the operation of the system.

(5)   In subsection (4)—

'public funds' includes funds provided by any Community institution;

'relevant authority' means—

    (a)   a government department,

    (b)   a local authority, or

    (c)   any other authority administering housing benefit or council tax benefit.

30.   Health, education and social work

(1)   The Secretary of State may by order exempt from the subject information provisions, or modify those provisions in relation to, personal data consisting of information as to the physical or mental health or condition of the data subject.

(2)   The Secretary of State may by order exempt from the subject information provisions, or modify those provisions in relation to—

    (a)   personal data in respect of which the data controller is the proprietor of, or a teacher at, a school, and which consist of information relating to persons who are or have been pupils at the school, or

    (b)   personal data in respect of which the data controller is an education authority in Scotland, and which consist of information relating to persons who are receiving, or have received, further education provided by the authority.

(3)   The Secretary of State may by order exempt from the subject information provisions, or modify those provisions in relation to, personal data of such other descriptions as may be specified in the order, being information—

    (a)   processed by government departments or local authorities or by voluntary organisations or other bodies designated by or under the order, and

    (b)   appearing to him to be processed in the course of, or for the purposes of, carrying out social work in relation to the data subject or other individuals;

but the Secretary of State shall not under this subsection confer any exemption or make any modification except so far as he considers that the application to the data of those provisions (or of those provisions without modification) would be likely to prejudice the carrying out of social work.

(4)   An order under this section may make different provision in relation to data consisting of information of different descriptions.

(5)   In this section—

'education authority' and 'further education' have the same meaning as in the Education (Scotland) Act 1980 ('the 1980 Act'), and

'proprietor'—

   (a)   in relation to a school in England or Wales, has the same meaning as in the Education Act 1996,

   (b)   in relation to a school in Scotland, means—

      (i)   in the case of a self-governing school, the board of management within the meaning of the Self-Governing Schools etc. (Scotland) Act 1989,

      (ii)   in the case of an independent school, the proprietor within the meaning of the 1980 Act,

      (iii)   in the case of a grant-aided school, the managers within the meaning of the 1980 Act, and

      (iv)   in the case of a public school, the education authority within the meaning of the 1980 Act, and

   (c)   in relation to a school in Northern Ireland, has the same meaning as in the Education and Libraries (Northern Ireland) Order 1986 and includes, in the case of a controlled school, the Board of Governors of the school.

31.   Regulatory activity

(1)   Personal data processed for the purposes of discharging functions to which this subsection applies are exempt from the subject information provisions in any case to the extent to which the application of those provisions to the data would be likely to prejudice the proper discharge of those functions.

(2)   Subsection (1) applies to any relevant function which is designed—

   (a)   for protecting members of the public against—

      (i)   financial loss due to dishonesty, malpractice or other seriously improper conduct by, or the unfitness or incompetence of, persons concerned in the provision of banking, insurance, investment or other financial services or in the management of bodies corporate,

      (ii)   financial loss due to the conduct of discharged or undischarged bankrupts, or

      (iii)   dishonesty, malpractice or other seriously improper conduct by, or the unfitness or incompetence of, persons authorised to carry on any profession or other activity,

   (b)   for protecting charities against misconduct or mismanagement (whether by trustees or other persons) in their administration,

   (c)   for protecting the property of charities from loss or misapplication,

   (d)   for the recovery of the property of charities,

   (e)   for securing the health, safety and welfare of persons at work, or

   (f)   for protecting persons other than persons at work against risk to health or safety arising out of or in connection with the actions of persons at work.

(3)   In subsection (2) 'relevant function' means—

   (a)   any function conferred on any person by or under any enactment,

   (b)   any function of the Crown, a Minister of the Crown or a government department, or

(c)   any other function which is of a public nature and is exercised in the public interest.

(4)   Personal data processed for the purpose of discharging any function which—

(a)   is conferred by or under any enactment on—

(i)   the Parliamentary Commissioner for Administration,

(ii)   the Commission for Local Administration in England, the Commission for Local Administration in Wales or the Commissioner for Local Administration in Scotland,

(iii)   the Health Service Commissioner for England, the Health Service Commissioner for Wales or the Health Service Commissioner for Scotland,

(iv)   the Welsh Administration Ombudsman,

(v)   the Assembly Ombudsman for Northern Ireland, or

(vi)   the Northern Ireland Commissioner for Complaints, and

(b)   is designed for protecting members of the public against—

(i)   maladministration by public bodies,

(ii)   failures in services provided by public bodies, or

(iii)   a failure of a public body to provide a service which it was a function of the body to provide,

are exempt from the subject information provisions in any case to the extent to which the application of those provisions to the data would be likely to prejudice the proper discharge of that function.

(5)   Personal data processed for the purpose of discharging any function which—

(a)   is conferred by or under any enactment on the Director General of Fair Trading, and

(b)   is designed—

(i)   for protecting members of the public against conduct which may adversely affect their interests by persons carrying on a business,

(ii)   for regulating agreements or conduct which have as their object or effect the prevention, restriction or distortion of competition in connection with any commercial activity, or

(iii)   for regulating conduct on the part of one or more undertakings which amounts to the abuse of a dominant position in a market,

are exempt from the subject information provisions in any case to the extent to which the application of those provisions to the data would be likely to prejudice the proper discharge of that function.

32.   Journalism, literature and art

(1)   Personal data which are processed only for the special purposes are exempt from any provision to which this subsection relates if—

(a)   the processing is undertaken with a view to the publication by any person of any journalistic, literary or artistic material,

(b)   the data controller reasonably believes that, having regard in particular to the special importance of the public interest in freedom of expression, publication would be in the public interest, and

(c)   the data controller reasonably believes that, in all the circumstances, compliance with that provision is incompatible with the special purposes.

(2)   Subsection (1) relates to the provisions of—

(a)   the data protection principles except the seventh data protection principle,

    (b)   section 7,

    (c)   section 10,

    (d)   section 12, and

    (e)   section 14(1) to (3).

(3)   In considering for the purposes of subsection (1)(b) whether the belief of a data controller that publication would be in the public interest was or is a reasonable one, regard may be had to his compliance with any code of practice which—

    (a)   is relevant to the publication in question, and

    (b)   is designated by the Secretary of State by order for the purposes of this subsection.

(4)   Where at any time ('the relevant time') in any proceedings against a data controller under section 7(9), 10(4), 12(8) or 14 or by virtue of section 13 the data controller claims, or it appears to the court, that any personal data to which the proceedings relate are being processed—

    (a)   only for the special purposes, and

    (b)   with a view to the publication by any person of any journalistic, literary or artistic material which, at the time twenty-four hours immediately before the relevant time, had not previously been published by the data controller,

the court shall stay the proceedings until either of the conditions in subsection (5) is met.

(5)   Those conditions are—

    (a)   that a determination of the Commissioner under section 45 with respect to the data in question takes effect, or

    (b)   in a case where the proceedings were stayed on the making of a claim, that the claim is withdrawn.

(6)   For the purposes of this Act 'publish', in relation to journalistic, literary or artistic material, means make available to the public or any section of the public.

33.   Research, history and statistics

(1)   In this section—

'research purposes' includes statistical or historical purposes;

'the relevant conditions', in relation to any processing of personal data, means the conditions—

    (a)   that the data are not processed to support measures or decisions with respect to particular individuals, and

    (b)   that the data are not processed in such a way that substantial damage or substantial distress is, or is likely to be, caused to any data subject.

(2)   For the purposes of the second data protection principle, the further processing of personal data only for research purposes in compliance with the relevant conditions is not to be regarded as incompatible with the purposes for which they were obtained.

(3)   Personal data which are processed only for research purposes in compliance with the relevant conditions may, notwithstanding the fifth data protection principle, be kept indefinitely.

(4)   Personal data which are processed only for research purposes are exempt from section 7 if—

    (a)   they are processed in compliance with the relevant conditions, and

    (b)   the results of the research or any resulting statistics are not made available in a form which identifies data subjects or any of them.

(5)   For the purposes of subsections (2) to (4) personal data are not to be treated as processed otherwise than for research purposes merely because the data are disclosed—

    (a)   to any person, for research purposes only,

    (b)   to the data subject or a person acting on his behalf,

    (c)   at the request, or with the consent, of the data subject or a person acting on his behalf, or

    (d)   in circumstances in which the person making the disclosure has reasonable grounds for believing that the disclosure falls within paragraph (a), (b) or (c).

34.   Information available to the public by or under enactment

Personal data are exempt from—

    (a)   the subject information provisions,

    (b)   the fourth data protection principle and section 14(1) to (3), and

    (c)   the non-disclosure provisions,

if the data consist of information which the data controller is obliged by or under any enactment to make available to the public, whether by publishing it, by making it available for inspection, or otherwise and whether gratuitously or on payment of a fee.

35.   Disclosures required by law or made in connection with legal proceedings etc.

(1)   Personal data are exempt from the non-disclosure provisions where the disclosure is required by or under any enactment, by any rule of law or by the order of a court.

(2)   Personal data are exempt from the non-disclosure provisions where the disclosure is necessary—

    (a)   for the purpose of, or in connection with, any legal proceedings (including prospective legal proceedings), or

    (b)   for the purpose of obtaining legal advice,

or is otherwise necessary for the purposes of establishing, exercising or defending legal rights.

36.   Domestic purposes

Personal data processed by an individual only for the purposes of that individual's personal, family or household affairs (including recreational purposes) are exempt from the data protection principles and the provisions of Parts II and III.

37.   Miscellaneous exemptions

Schedule 7 (which confers further miscellaneous exemptions) has effect.

38.   Powers to make further exemptions by order

(1)   The Secretary of State may by order exempt from the subject information provisions personal data consisting of information the disclosure of which is prohibited or restricted by or under any enactment if and to the extent that he considers it necessary for the safeguarding of the interests of the data subject or the rights and freedoms of any other individual that the prohibition or restriction ought to prevail over those provisions.

(2)   The Secretary of State may by order exempt from the non-disclosure provisions any disclosures of personal data made in circumstances specified in the order, if he considers the exemption is necessary for the safeguarding of the interests of the data subject or the rights and freedoms of any other individual.

39.   Transitional relief
Schedule 8 (which confers transitional exemptions) has effect.

PART V
ENFORCEMENT

40.   Enforcement notices
(1)   If the Commissioner is satisfied that a data controller has contravened or is contravening any of the data protection principles, the Commissioner may serve him with a notice (in this Act referred to as 'an enforcement notice') requiring him, for complying with the principle or principles in question, to do either or both of the following—
(a)   to take within such time as may be specified in the notice, or to refrain from taking after such time as may be so specified, such steps as are so specified, or
(b)   to refrain from processing any personal data, or any personal data of a description specified in the notice, or to refrain from processing them for a purpose so specified or in a manner so specified, after such time as may be so specified.
(2)   In deciding whether to serve an enforcement notice, the Commissioner shall consider whether the contravention has caused or is likely to cause any person damage or distress.
(3)   An enforcement notice in respect of a contravention of the fourth data protection principle which requires the data controller to rectify, block, erase or destroy any inaccurate data may also require the data controller to rectify, block, erase or destroy any other data held by him and containing an expression of opinion which appears to the Commissioner to be based on the inaccurate data.
(4)   An enforcement notice in respect of a contravention of the fourth data protection principle, in the case of data which accurately record information received or obtained by the data controller from the data subject or a third party, may require the data controller either—
(a)   to rectify, block, erase or destroy any inaccurate data and any other data held by him and containing an expression of opinion as mentioned in subsection (3), or
(b)   to take such steps as are specified in the notice for securing compliance with the requirements specified in paragraph 7 of Part II of Schedule 1 and, if the Commissioner thinks fit, for supplementing the data with such statement of the true facts relating to the matters dealt with by the data as the Commissioner may approve.
(5)   Where—
(a)   an enforcement notice requires the data controller to rectify, block, erase or destroy any personal data, or
(b)   the Commissioner is satisfied that personal data which have been rectified, blocked, erased or destroyed had been processed in contravention of any of the data protection principles,
an enforcement notice may, if reasonably practicable, require the data controller to notify third parties to whom the data have been disclosed of the rectification, blocking, erasure or destruction; and in determining whether it is reasonably practicable to require such notification regard shall be had, in particular, to the number of persons who would have to be notified.
(6)   An enforcement notice must contain—

(a)   a statement of the data protection principle or principles which the Commissioner is satisfied have been or are being contravened and his reasons for reaching that conclusion, and

(b)   particulars of the rights of appeal conferred by section 48.

(7)   Subject to subsection (8), an enforcement notice must not require any of the provisions of the notice to be complied with before the end of the period within which an appeal can be brought against the notice and, if such an appeal is brought, the notice need not be complied with pending the determination or withdrawal of the appeal.

(8)   If by reason of special circumstances the Commissioner considers that an enforcement notice should be complied with as a matter of urgency he may include in the notice a statement to that effect and a statement of his reasons for reaching that conclusion; and in that event subsection (7) shall not apply but the notice must not require the provisions of the notice to be complied with before the end of the period of seven days beginning with the day on which the notice is served.

(9)   Notification regulations (as defined by section 16(2)) may make provision as to the effect of the service of an enforcement notice on any entry in the register maintained under section 19 which relates to the person on whom the notice is served.

(10)   This section has effect subject to section 46(1).

41.   Cancellation of enforcement notice

(1)   If the Commissioner considers that all or any of the provisions of an enforcement notice need not be complied with in order to ensure compliance with the data protection principle or principles to which it relates, he may cancel or vary the notice by written notice to the person on whom it was served.

(2)   A person on whom an enforcement notice has been served may, at any time after the expiry of the period during which an appeal can be brought against that notice, apply in writing to the Commissioner for the cancellation or variation of that notice on the ground that, by reason of a change of circumstances, all or any of the provisions of that notice need not be complied with in order to ensure compliance with the data protection principle or principles to which that notice relates.

42.   Request for assessment

(1)   A request may be made to the Commissioner by or on behalf of any person who is, or believes himself to be, directly affected by any processing of personal data for an assessment as to whether it is likely or unlikely that the processing has been or is being carried out in compliance with the provisions of this Act.

(2)   On receiving a request under this section, the Commissioner shall make an assessment in such manner as appears to him to be appropriate, unless he has not been supplied with such information as he may reasonably require in order to—

(a)   satisfy himself as to the identity of the person making the request, and

(b)   enable him to identify the processing in question.

(3)   The matters to which the Commissioner may have regard in determining in what manner it is appropriate to make an assessment include—

(a)   the extent to which the request appears to him to raise a matter of substance,

(b)   any undue delay in making the request, and

(c)   whether or not the person making the request is entitled to make an application under section 7 in respect of the personal data in question.

(4) Where the Commissioner has received a request under this section he shall notify the person who made the request—

(a) whether he has made an assessment as a result of the request, and

(b) to the extent that he considers appropriate, having regard in particular to any exemption from section 7 applying in relation to the personal data concerned, of any view formed or action taken as a result of the request.

43. Information notices

(1) If the Commissioner—

(a) has received a request under section 42 in respect of any processing of personal data, or

(b) reasonably requires any information for the purpose of determining whether the data controller has complied or is complying with the data protection principles,

he may serve the data controller with a notice (in this Act referred to as 'an information notice') requiring the data controller, within such time as is specified in the notice, to furnish the Commissioner, in such form as may be so specified, with such information relating to the request or to compliance with the principles as is so specified.

(2) An information notice must contain—

(a) In a case falling within subsection (1)(a), a statement that the Commissioner has received a request under section 42 in relation to the specified processing, or

(b) in a case falling within subsection (1)(b), a statement that the Commissioner regards the specified information as relevant for the purpose of determining whether the data controller has complied, or is complying, with the data protection principles and his reasons for regarding it as relevant for that purpose.

(3) An information notice must also contain particulars of the rights of appeal conferred by section 48.

(4) Subject to subsection (5), the time specified in an information notice shall not expire before the end of the period within which an appeal can be brought against the notice and, if such an appeal is brought, the information need not be furnished pending the determination or withdrawal of the appeal.

(5) If by reason of special circumstances the Commissioner considers that the information is required as a matter of urgency, he may include in the notice a statement to that effect and a statement of his reasons for reaching that conclusion; and in that event subsection (4) shall not apply, but the notice shall not require the information to be furnished before the end of the period of seven days beginning with the day on which the notice is served.

(6) A person shall not be required by virtue of this section to furnish the Commissioner with any information in respect of—

(a) any communication between a professional legal adviser and his client in connection with the giving of legal advice to the client with respect to his obligations, liabilities or rights under this Act, or

(b) any communication between a professional legal adviser and his client, or between such an adviser or his client and any other person, made in connection with or in contemplation of proceedings under or arising out of this Act (including proceedings before the Tribunal) and for the purposes of such proceedings.

(7)   In subsection (6) references to the client of a professional legal adviser include references to any person representing such a client.

(8)   A person shall not be required by virtue of this section to furnish the Commissioner with any information if the furnishing of that information would, by revealing evidence of the commission of any offence other than an offence under this Act, expose him to proceedings for that offence.

(9)   The Commissioner may cancel an information notice by written notice to the person on whom it was served.

(10)   This section has effect subject to section 46(3).

44.   Special information notices

(1)   If the Commissioner—

(a)   has received a request under section 42 in respect of any processing of personal data, or

(b)   has reasonable grounds for suspecting that, in a case in which proceedings have been stayed under section 32, the personal data to which the proceedings relate—

(i)   are not being processed only for the special purposes, or

(ii)   are not being processed with a view to the publication by any person of any journalistic, literary or artistic material which has not previously been published by the data controller,

he may serve the data controller with a notice (in this Act referred to as a 'special information notice') requiring the data controller, within such time as is specified in the notice, to furnish the Commissioner, in such form as may be so specified, with such information as is so specified for the purpose specified in subsection (2).

(2)   That purpose is the purpose of ascertaining—

(a)   whether the personal data are being processed only for the special purposes, or

(b)   whether they are being processed with a view to the publication by any person of any journalistic, literary or artistic material which has not previously been published by the data controller.

(3)   A special information notice must contain—

(a)   in a case falling within paragraph (a) of subsection (1), a statement that the Commissioner has received a request under section 42 in relation to the specified processing, or

(b)   in a case falling within paragraph (b) of that subsection, a statement of the Commissioner's grounds for suspecting that the personal data are not being processed as mentioned in that paragraph.

(4)   A special information notice must also contain particulars of the rights of appeal conferred by section 48.

(5)   Subject to subsection (6), the time specified in a special information notice shall not expire before the end of the period within which an appeal can be brought against the notice and, if such an appeal is brought, the information need not be furnished pending the determination or withdrawal of the appeal.

(6)   If by reason of special circumstances the Commissioner considers that the information is required as a matter of urgency, he may include in the notice a statement to that effect and a statement of his reasons for reaching that conclusion; and in that event subsection (5) shall not apply, but the notice shall not require the

information to be furnished before the end of the period of seven days beginning with the day on which the notice is served.

(7)   A person shall not be required by virtue of this section to furnish the Commissioner with any information in respect of—

(a)   any communication between a professional legal adviser and his client in connection with the giving of legal advice to the client with respect to his obligations, liabilities or rights under this Act, or

(b)   any communication between a professional legal adviser and his client, or between such an adviser or his client and any other person, made in connection with or in contemplation of proceedings under or arising out of this Act (including proceedings before the Tribunal) and for the purposes of such proceedings.

(8)   In subsection (7) references to the client of a professional legal adviser include references to any person representing such a client.

(9)   A person shall not be required by virtue of this section to furnish the Commissioner with any information if the furnishing of that information would, by revealing evidence of the commission of any offence other than an offence under this Act, expose him to proceedings for that offence.

(10)   The Commissioner may cancel a special information notice by written notice to the person on whom it was served.

45.   Determination by Commissioner as to the special purposes

(1)   Where at any time it appears to the Commissioner (whether as a result of the service of a special information notice or otherwise) that any personal data—

(a)   are not being processed only for the special purposes, or

(b)   are not being processed with a view to the publication by any person of any journalistic, literary or artistic material which has not previously been published by the data controller,

he may make a determination in writing to that effect.

(2)   Notice of the determination shall be given to the data controller; and the notice must contain particulars of the right of appeal conferred by section 48.

(3)   A determination under subsection (1) shall not take effect until the end of the period within which an appeal can be brought and, where an appeal is brought, shall not take effect pending the determination or withdrawal of the appeal.

46.   Restriction on enforcement in case of processing for the special purposes

(1)   The Commissioner may not at any time serve an enforcement notice on a data controller with respect to the processing of personal data for the special purposes unless—

(a)   a determination under section 45(1) with respect to those data has taken effect, and

(b)   the court has granted leave for the notice to be served.

(2)   The court shall not grant leave for the purposes of subsection (1)(b) unless it is satisfied—

(a)   that the Commissioner has reason to suspect a contravention of the data protection principles which is of substantial public importance, and

(b)   except where the case is one of urgency, that the data controller has been given notice, in accordance with rules of court, of the application for leave.

(3)   The Commissioner may not serve an information notice on a data controller with respect to the processing of personal data for the special purposes unless a determination under section 45(1) with respect to those data has taken effect.

47.   Failure to comply with notice

(1)   A person who fails to comply with an enforcement notice, an information notice or a special information notice is guilty of an offence.

(2)   A person who, in purported compliance with an information notice or a special information notice—

(a)   makes a statement which he knows to be false in a material respect, or

(b)   recklessly makes a statement which is false in a material respect, is guilty of an offence.

(3)   It is a defence for a person charged with an offence under subsection (1) to prove that he exercised all due diligence to comply with the notice in question.

48.   Rights of appeal

(1)   A person on whom an enforcement notice, an information notice or a special information notice has been served may appeal to the Tribunal against the notice.

(2)   A person on whom an enforcement notice has been served may appeal to the Tribunal against the refusal of an application under section 41(2) for cancellation or variation of the notice.

(3)   Where an enforcement notice, an information notice or a special information notice contains a statement by the Commissioner in accordance with section 40(8), 43(5) or 44(6) then, whether or not the person appeals against the notice, he may appeal against—

(a)   the Commissioner's decision to include the statement in the notice, or

(b)   the effect of the inclusion of the statement as respects any part of the notice.

(4)   A data controller in respect of whom a determination has been made under section 45 may appeal to the Tribunal against the determination.

(5)   Schedule 6 has effect in relation to appeals under this section and the proceedings of the Tribunal in respect of any such appeal.

49.   Determination of appeals

(1)   If on an appeal under section 48(1) the Tribunal considers—

(a)   that the notice against which the appeal is brought is not in accordance with the law, or

(b)   to the extent that the notice involved an exercise of discretion by the Commissioner, that he ought to have exercised his discretion differently,

the Tribunal shall allow the appeal or substitute such other notice or decision as could have been served or made by the Commissioner; and in any other case the Tribunal shall dismiss the appeal.

(2)   On such an appeal, the Tribunal may review any determination of fact on which the notice in question was based.

(3)   If on an appeal under section 48(2) the Tribunal considers that the enforcement notice ought to be cancelled or varied by reason of a change in circumstances, the Tribunal shall cancel or vary the notice.

(4)   On an appeal under subsection (3) of section 48 the Tribunal may direct—

(a)   that the notice in question shall have effect as if it did not contain any such statement as is mentioned in that subsection, or

(b)   that the inclusion of the statement shall not have effect in relation to any part of the notice,

and may make such modifications in the notice as may be required for giving effect to the direction.

(5)   On an appeal under section 48(4), the Tribunal may cancel the determination of the Commissioner.

(6)   Any party to an appeal to the Tribunal under section 48 may appeal from the decision of the Tribunal on a point of law to the appropriate court; and that court shall be—

(a)   the High Court of Justice in England if the address of the person who was the appellant before the Tribunal is in England or Wales,

(b)   the Court of Session if that address is in Scotland, and

(c)   the High Court of Justice in Northern Ireland if that address is in Northern Ireland.

(7)   For the purposes of subsection (6)—

(a)   the address of a registered company is that of its registered office, and

(b)   the address of a person (other than a registered company) carrying on a business is that of his principal place of business in the United Kingdom.

50.   Powers of entry and inspection

Schedule 9 (powers of entry and inspection) has effect.

PART VI
MISCELLANEOUS AND GENERAL

Functions of Commissioner

51.   General duties of Commissioner

(1)   It shall be the duty of the Commissioner to promote the following of good practice by data controllers and, in particular, so to perform his functions under this Act as to promote the observance of the requirements of this Act by data controllers.

(2)   The Commissioner shall arrange for the dissemination in such form and manner as he considers appropriate of such information as it may appear to him expedient to give to the public about the operation of this Act, about good practice, and about other matters within the scope of his functions under this Act, and may give advice to any person as to any of those matters.

(3)   Where—

(a)   the Secretary of State so directs by order, or

(b)   the Commissioner considers it appropriate to do so,

the Commissioner shall, after such consultation with trade associations, data subjects or persons representing data subjects as appears to him to be appropriate, prepare and disseminate to such persons as he considers appropriate codes of practice for guidance as to good practice.

(4)   The Commissioner shall also—

(a)   where he considers it appropriate to do so, encourage trade associations to prepare, and to disseminate to their members, such codes of practice, and

(b) where any trade association submits a code of practice to him for his consideration, consider the code and, after such consultation with data subjects or persons representing data subjects as appears to him to be appropriate, notify the trade association whether in his opinion the code promotes the following of good practice.

(5) An order under subsection (3) shall describe the personal data or processing to which the code of practice is to relate, and may also describe the persons or classes of persons to whom it is to relate.

(6) The Commissioner shall arrange for the dissemination in such form and manner as he considers appropriate of—

(a) any Community finding as defined by paragraph 15(2) of Part II of Schedule 1,

(b) any decision of the European Commission, under the procedure provided for in Article 31(2) of the Data Protection Directive, which is made for the purposes of Article 26(3) or (4) of the Directive, and

(c) such other information as it may appear to him to be expedient to give to data controllers in relation to any personal data about the protection of the rights and freedoms of data subjects in relation to the processing of personal data in countries and territories outside the European Economic Area.

(7) The Commissioner may, with the consent of the data controller, assess any processing of personal data for the following of good practice and shall inform the data controller of the results of the assessment.

(8) The Commissioner may charge such sums as he may with the consent of the Secretary of State determine for any services provided by the Commissioner by virtue of this Part.

(9) In this section—

'good practice' means such practice in the processing of personal data as appears to the Commissioner to be desirable having regard to the interests of data subjects and others, and includes (but is not limited to) compliance with the requirements of this Act;

'trade association' includes any body representing data controllers.

52. Reports and codes of practice to be laid before Parliament

(1) The Commissioner shall lay annually before each House of Parliament a general report on the exercise of his functions under this Act.

(2) The Commissioner may from time to time lay before each House of Parliament such other reports with respect to those functions as he thinks fit.

(3) The Commissioner shall lay before each House of Parliament any code of practice prepared under section 51(3) for complying with a direction of the Secretary of State, unless the code is included in any report laid under subsection (1) or (2).

53. Assistance by Commissioner in cases involving processing for the special purposes

(1) An individual who is an actual or prospective party to any proceedings under section 7(9), 10(4), 12(8) or 14 or by virtue of section 13 which relate to personal data processed for the special purposes may apply to the Commissioner for assistance in relation to those proceedings.

(2)   The Commissioner shall, as soon as reasonably practicable after receiving an application under subsection (1), consider it and decide whether and to what extent to grant it, but he shall not grant the application unless, in his opinion, the case involves a matter of substantial public importance.

(3)   If the Commissioner decides to provide assistance, he shall, as soon as reasonably practicable after making the decision, notify the applicant, stating the extent of the assistance to be provided.

(4)   If the Commissioner decides not to provide assistance, he shall, as soon as reasonably practicable after making the decision, notify the applicant of his decision and, if he thinks fit, the reasons for it.

(5)   In this section—

(a)   references to 'proceedings' include references to prospective proceedings, and

(b)   'applicant', in relation to assistance under this section, means an individual who applies for assistance.

(6)   Schedule 10 has effect for supplementing this section.

54.   International co-operation

(1)   The Commissioner—

(a)   shall continue to be the designated authority in the United Kingdom for the purposes of Article 13 of the Convention, and

(b)   shall be the supervisory authority in the United Kingdom for the purposes of the Data Protection Directive.

(2)   The Secretary of State may by order make provision as to the functions to be discharged by the Commissioner as the designated authority in the United Kingdom for the purposes of Article 13 of the Convention.

(3)   The Secretary of State may by order make provision as to co-operation by the Commissioner with the European Commission and with supervisory authorities in other EEA States in connection with the performance of their respective duties and, in particular, as to—

(a)   the exchange of information with supervisory authorities in other EEA States or with the European Commission, and

(b)   the exercise within the United Kingdom at the request of a supervisory authority in another EEA State, in cases excluded by section 5 from the application of the other provisions of this Act, of functions of the Commissioner specified in the order.

(4)   The Commissioner shall also carry out any data protection functions which the Secretary of State may by order direct him to carry out for the purpose of enabling Her Majesty's Government in the United Kingdom to give effect to any international obligations of the United Kingdom.

(5)   The Commissioner shall, if so directed by the Secretary of State, provide any authority exercising data protection functions under the law of a colony specified in the direction with such assistance in connection with the discharge of those functions as the Secretary of State may direct or approve, on such terms (including terms as to payment) as the Secretary of State may direct or approve.

(6)   Where the European Commission makes a decision for the purposes of Article 26(3) or (4) of the Data Protection Directive under the procedure provided for in Article 31(2) of the Directive, the Commissioner shall comply with that

decision in exercising his functions under paragraph 9 of Schedule 4 or, as the case may be, paragraph 8 of that Schedule.

(7)   The Commissioner shall inform the European Commission and the supervisory authorities in other EEA States—

(a)   of any approvals granted for the purposes of paragraph 8 of Schedule 4, and

(b)   of any authorisations granted for the purposes of paragraph 9 of that Schedule.

(8)   In this section—

'the Convention' means the Convention for the Protection of Individuals with regard to Automatic Processing of Personal Data which was opened for signature on 28th January 1981;

'data protection functions' means functions relating to the protection of individuals with respect to the processing of personal information.

Unlawful obtaining etc. of personal data

55.   Unlawful obtaining etc. of personal data

(1)   A person must not knowingly or recklessly, without the consent of the data controller—

(a)   obtain or disclose personal data or the information contained in personal data, or

(b)   procure the disclosure to another person of the information contained in personal data.

(2)   Subsection (1) does not apply to a person who shows—

(a)   that the obtaining, disclosing or procuring—

(i)   was necessary for the purpose of preventing or detecting crime, or

(ii)   was required or authorised by or under any enactment, by any rule of law or by the order of a court,

(b)   that he acted in the reasonable belief that he had in law the right to obtain or disclose the data or information or, as the case may be, to procure the disclosure of the information to the other person,

(c)   that he acted in the reasonable belief that he would have had the consent of the data controller if the data controller had known of the obtaining, disclosing or procuring and the circumstances of it, or

(d)   that in the particular circumstances the obtaining, disclosing or procuring was justified as being in the public interest.

(3)   A person who contravenes subsection (1) is guilty of an offence.

(4)   A person who sells personal data is guilty of an offence if he has obtained the data in contravention of subsection (1).

(5)   A person who offers to sell personal data is guilty of an offence if—

(a)   he has obtained the data in contravention of subsection (1), or

(b)   he subsequently obtains the data in contravention of that subsection.

(6)   For the purposes of subsection (5), an advertisement indicating that personal data are or may be for sale is an offer to sell the data.

(7)   Section 1(2) does not apply for the purposes of this section; and for the purposes of subsections (4) to (6), 'personal data' includes information extracted from personal data.

(8)   References in this section to personal data do not include references to personal data which by virtue of section 28 are exempt from this section.

Records obtained under data subject's right of access

56.   Prohibition of requirement as to production of certain records

(1)   A person must not, in connection with—

    (a)   the recruitment of another person as an employee,

    (b)   the continued employment of another person, or

    (c)   any contract for the provision of services to him by another person,

require that other person or a third party to supply him with a relevant record or to produce a relevant record to him.

(2)   A person concerned with the provision (for payment or not) of goods, facilities or services to the public or a section of the public must not, as a condition of providing or offering to provide any goods, facilities or services to another person, require that other person or a third party to supply him with a relevant record or to produce a relevant record to him.

(3)   Subsections (1) and (2) do not apply to a person who shows—

    (a)   that the imposition of the requirement was required or authorised by or under any enactment, by any rule of law or by the order of a court, or

    (b)   that in the particular circumstances the imposition of the requirement was justified as being in the public interest.

(4)   Having regard to the provisions of Part V of the Police Act 1997 (certificates of criminal records etc.), the imposition of the requirement referred to in subsection (1) or (2) is not to be regarded as being justified as being in the public interest on the ground that it would assist in the prevention or detection of crime.

(5)   A person who contravenes subsection (1) or (2) is guilty of an offence.

(6)   In this section 'a relevant record' means any record which—

    (a)   has been or is to be obtained by a data subject from any data controller specified in the first column of the Table below in the exercise of the right conferred by section 7, and

    (b)   contains information relating to any matter specified in relation to that data controller in the second column,

and includes a copy of such a record or a part of such a record.

TABLE

Data controller	Subject-matter
1. Any of the following persons— (a) a chief officer of police of a police force in England and Wales. (b) a chief constable of a police force in Scotland. (c) the Chief Constable of the Royal Ulster Constabulary. (d) the Director General of the National Criminal Intelligence Service. (e) the Director General of the National Crime Squad.	(a) Convictions. (b) Cautions.
2. The Secretary of State.	(a) Convictions. (b) Cautions. (c) His functions under section 53 of the Children and Young Persons Act 1933, section 205(2) or 208 of the Criminal Procedure (Scotland) Act 1995 or section 73 of the Children and Young Persons Act (Northern Ireland) 1968 in relation to any person sentenced to detention. (d) His functions under the Prison Act 1952, the Prisons (Scotland) Act 1989 or the Prison Act (Northern Ireland) 1953 in relation to any person imprisoned or detained. (e) His functions under the Social Security Contributions and Benefits Act 1992, the Social Security Administration Act 1992 or the Jobseekers Act 1995. (f) His functions under Part V of the Police Act 1997.
3. The Department of Health and Social Services for Northern Ireland.	Its functions under the Social Security Contributions and Benefits (Northern Ireland) Act 1992, the Social Security Administration (Northern Ireland) Act 1992 or the Jobseekers (Northern Ireland) Order 1995.

(7)   In the Table in subsection (6)—

'caution' means a caution given to any person in England and Wales or Northern Ireland in respect of an offence which, at the time when the caution is given, is admitted;

'conviction' has the same meaning as in the Rehabilitation of Offenders Act 1974 or the Rehabilitation of Offenders (Northern Ireland) Order 1978.

(8)   The Secretary of State may by order amend—

(a)   the Table in subsection (6), and

(b)   subsection (7).

(9)   For the purposes of this section a record which states that a data controller is not processing any personal data relating to a particular matter shall be taken to be a record containing information relating to that matter.

(10)   In this section 'employee' means an individual who—

(a)   works under a contract of employment, as defined by section 230(2) of the Employment Rights Act 1996, or

(b)   holds any office,

whether or not he is entitled to remuneration; and 'employment' shall be construed accordingly.

57.   Avoidance of certain contractual terms relating to health records

(1)   Any term or condition of a contract is void in so far as it purports to require an individual—

(a)   to supply any other person with a record to which this section applies, or with a copy of such a record or a part of such a record, or

(b)   to produce to any other person such a record, copy or part.

(2)   This section applies to any record which—

(a)   has been or is to be obtained by a data subject in the exercise of the right conferred by section 7, and

(b)   consists of the information contained in any health record as defined by section 68(2).

Information provided to Commissioner or Tribunal

58.   Disclosure of information

No enactment or rule of law prohibiting or restricting the disclosure of information shall preclude a person from furnishing the Commissioner or the Tribunal with any information necessary for the discharge of their functions under this Act.

59.   Confidentiality of information

(1)   No person who is or has been the Commissioner, a member of the Commissioner's staff or an agent of the Commissioner shall disclose any information which—

(a)   has been obtained by, or furnished to, the Commissioner under or for the purposes of this Act,

(b)   relates to an identified or identifiable individual or business, and

(c)   is not at the time of the disclosure, and has not previously been, available to the public from other sources,

unless the disclosure is made with lawful authority.

(2)   For the purposes of subsection (1) a disclosure of information is made with lawful authority only if, and to the extent that—

    (a)   the disclosure is made with the consent of the individual or of the person for the time being carrying on the business,

    (b)   the information was provided for the purpose of its being made available to the public (in whatever manner) under any provision of this Act,

    (c)   the disclosure is made for the purposes of, and is necessary for, the discharge of—

        (i)   any functions under this Act, or

        (ii)   any Community obligation,

    (d)   the disclosure is made for the purposes of any proceedings, whether criminal or civil and whether arising under, or by virtue of, this Act or otherwise, or

    (e)   having regard to the rights and freedoms or legitimate interests of any person, the disclosure is necessary in the public interest.

(3)   Any person who knowingly or recklessly discloses information in contravention of subsection (1) is guilty of an offence.

General provisions relating to offences

60. Prosecutions and penalties

(1)   No proceedings for an offence under this Act shall be instituted—

    (a)   in England or Wales, except by the Commissioner or by or with the consent of the Director of Public Prosecutions;

    (b)   in Northern Ireland, except by the Commissioner or by or with the consent of the Director of Public Prosecutions for Northern Ireland.

(2)   A person guilty of an offence under any provision of this Act other than paragraph 12 of Schedule 9 is liable—

    (a)   on summary conviction, to a fine not exceeding the statutory maximum, or

    (b)   on conviction on indictment, to a fine.

(3)   A person guilty of an offence under paragraph 12 of Schedule 9 is liable on summary conviction to a fine not exceeding level 5 on the standard scale.

(4)   Subject to subsection (5), the court by or before which a person is convicted of—

    (a)   an offence under section 21(1), 22(6), 55 or 56,

    (b)   an offence under section 21(2) relating to processing which is assessable processing for the purposes of section 22, or

    (c)   an offence under section 47(1) relating to an enforcement notice,

may order any document or other material used in connection with the processing of personal data and appearing to the court to be connected with the commission of the offence to be forfeited, destroyed or erased.

(5)   The court shall not make an order under subsection (4) in relation to any material where a person (other than the offender) claiming to be the owner of or otherwise interested in the material applies to be heard by the court, unless an opportunity is given to him to show cause why the order should not be made.

61. Liability of directors etc.

(1)   Where an offence under this Act has been committed by a body corporate and is proved to have been committed with the consent or connivance of or to be attributable to any neglect on the part of any director, manager, secretary or similar

officer of the body corporate or any person who was purporting to act in any such capacity, he as well as the body corporate shall be guilty of that offence and be liable to be proceeded against and punished accordingly.

(2)   Where the affairs of a body corporate are managed by its members subsection (1) shall apply in relation to the acts and defaults of a member in connection with his functions of management as if he were a director of the body corporate.

(3)   Where an offence under this Act has been committed by a Scottish partnership and the contravention in question is proved to have occurred with the consent or connivance of, or to be attributable to any neglect on the part of, a partner, he as well as the partnership shall be guilty of that offence and shall be liable to be proceeded against and punished accordingly.

Amendments of Consumer Credit Act 1974

62.   Amendments of Consumer Credit Act 1974

(1)   In section 158 of the Consumer Credit Act 1974 (duty of agency to disclose filed information)—

(a)   in subsection (1)—

(i)   in paragraph (a) for 'individual' there is substituted 'partnership or other unincorporated body of persons not consisting entirely of bodies corporate', and

(ii)   for 'him' there is substituted 'it',

(b)   in subsection (2), for 'his' there is substituted 'the consumer's', and

(c)   in subsection (3), for 'him' there is substituted 'the consumer'.

(2)   In section 159 of that Act (correction of wrong information) for subsection (1) there is substituted—

'(1)   Any individual (the 'objector') given—

(a)   information under section 7 of the Data Protection Act 1998 by a credit reference agency, or

(b)   information under section 158,

who considers that an entry in his file is incorrect, and that if it is not corrected he is likely to be prejudiced, may give notice to the agency requiring it either to remove the entry from the file or amend it.'

(3)   In subsections (2) to (6) of that section—

(a)   for 'consumer', wherever occurring, there is substituted 'objector', and

(b)   for 'Director', wherever occurring, there is substituted 'the relevant authority'.

(4)   After subsection (6) of that section there is inserted—

'(7)   The Data Protection Commissioner may vary or revoke any order made by him under this section.

(8)   In this section 'the relevant authority' means—

(a)   where the objector is a partnership or other unincorporated body of persons, the Director, and

(b)   in any other case, the Data Protection Commissioner.'

(5)   In section 160 of that Act (alternative procedure for business consumers)—

(a)   in subsection (4)—

(i)   for 'him' there is substituted 'to the consumer', and

(ii)   in paragraphs (a) and (b) for 'he' there is substituted 'the consumer' and for 'his' there is substituted 'the consumer's', and

(b)   after subsection (6) there is inserted—

'(7)　In this section 'consumer' has the same meaning as in section 158.'

General

63.　Application to Crown

(1)　This Act binds the Crown.

(2)　For the purposes of this Act each government department shall be treated as a person separate from any other government department.

(3)　Where the purposes for which and the manner in which any personal data are, or are to be, processed are determined by any person acting on behalf of the Royal Household, the Duchy of Lancaster or the Duchy of Cornwall, the data controller in respect of those data for the purposes of this Act shall be—

(a)　in relation to the Royal Household, the Keeper of the Privy Purse,

(b)　in relation to the Duchy of Lancaster, such person as the Chancellor of the Duchy appoints, and

(c)　in relation to the Duchy of Cornwall, such person as the Duke of Cornwall, or the possessor for the time being of the Duchy of Cornwall, appoints.

(4)　Different persons may be appointed under subsection (3)(b) or (c) for different purposes.

(5)　Neither a government department nor a person who is a data controller by virtue of subsection (3) shall be liable to prosecution under this Act, but section 55 and paragraph 12 of Schedule 9 shall apply to a person in the service of the Crown as they apply to any other person.

64.　Transmission of notices etc. by electronic or other means

(1)　This section applies to—

(a)　a notice or request under any provision of Part II,

(b)　a notice under subsection (1) of section 24 or particulars made available under that subsection, or

(c)　an application under section 41(2),

but does not apply to anything which is required to be served in accordance with rules of court.

(2)　The requirement that any notice, request, particulars or application to which this section applies should be in writing is satisfied where the text of the notice, request, particulars or application—

(a)　is transmitted by electronic means,

(b)　is received in legible form, and

(c)　is capable of being used for subsequent reference.

(3)　The Secretary of State may by regulations provide that any requirement that any notice, request, particulars or application to which this section applies should be in writing is not to apply in such circumstances as may be prescribed by the regulations.

65.　Service of notices by Commissioner

(1)　Any notice authorised or required by this Act to be served on or given to any person by the Commissioner may—

(a)　if that person is an individual, be served on him—

(i)　by delivering it to him, or

(ii)　by sending it to him by post addressed to him at his usual or last-known place of residence or business, or

(iii)   by leaving it for him at that place;

(b)   if that person is a body corporate or unincorporate, be served on that body—

(i)   by sending it by post to the proper officer of the body at its principal office, or

(ii)   by addressing it to the proper officer of the body and leaving it at that office;

(c)   if that person is a partnership in Scotland, be served on that partnership—

(i)   by sending it by post to the principal office of the partnership, or

(ii)   by addressing it to that partnership and leaving it at that office.

(2)   In subsection (1)(b) 'principal office', in relation to a registered company, means its registered office and 'proper officer', in relation to any body, means the secretary or other executive officer charged with the conduct of its general affairs.

(3)   This section is without prejudice to any other lawful method of serving or giving a notice.

66.   Exercise of rights in Scotland by children

(1)   Where a question falls to be determined in Scotland as to the legal capacity of a person under the age of sixteen years to exercise any right conferred by any provision of this Act, that person shall be taken to have that capacity where he has a general understanding of what it means to exercise that right.

(2)   Without prejudice to the generality of subsection (1), a person of twelve years of age or more shall be presumed to be of sufficient age and maturity to have such understanding as is mentioned in that subsection.

67.   Orders, regulations and rules

(1)   Any power conferred by this Act on the Secretary of State to make an order, regulations or rules shall be exercisable by statutory instrument.

(2)   Any order, regulations or rules made by the Secretary of State under this Act may—

(a)   make different provision for different cases, and

(b)   make such supplemental, incidental, consequential or transitional provision or savings as the Secretary of State considers appropriate;

and nothing in section 7(11), 19(5), 26(1) or 30(4) limits the generality of paragraph (a).

(3)   Before making—

(a)   an order under any provision of this Act other than section 75(3),

(b)   any regulations under this Act other than notification regulations (as defined by section 16(2)),

the Secretary of State shall consult the Commissioner.

(4)   A statutory instrument containing (whether alone or with other provisions) an order under—

section 10(2)(b),

section 12(5)(b),

section 22(1),

section 30,

section 32(3),

section 38,

section 56(8),

paragraph 10 of Schedule 3, or

paragraph 4 of Schedule 7,

shall not be made unless a draft of the instrument has been laid before and approved by a resolution of each House of Parliament.

(5) A statutory instrument which contains (whether alone or with other provisions)—

(a) an order under—

section 22(7),

section 23,

section 51(3),

section 54(2), (3) or (4),

paragraph 3, 4 or 14 of Part II of Schedule 1,

paragraph 6 of Schedule 2,

paragraph 2, 7 or 9 of Schedule 3,

paragraph 4 of Schedule 4,

paragraph 6 of Schedule 7,

(b) regulations under section 7 which—

(i) prescribe cases for the purposes of subsection (2)(b),

(ii) are made by virtue of subsection (7), or

(iii) relate to the definition of 'the prescribed period',

(c) regulations under section 8(1) or 9(3),

(d) regulations under section 64,

(e) notification regulations (as defined by section 16(2)), or

(f) rules under paragraph 7 of Schedule 6,

and which is not subject to the requirement in subsection (4) that a draft of the instrument be laid before and approved by a resolution of each House of Parliament, shall be subject to annulment in pursuance of a resolution of either House of Parliament.

(6) A statutory instrument which contains only—

(a) regulations prescribing fees for the purposes of any provision of this Act, or

(b) regulations under section 7 prescribing fees for the purposes of any other enactment,

shall be laid before Parliament after being made.

68. Meaning of 'accessible record'

(1) In this Act 'accessible record' means—

(a) a health record as defined by subsection (2),

(b) an educational record as defined by Schedule 11, or

(c) an accessible public record as defined by Schedule 12.

(2) In subsection (1)(a) 'health record' means any record which—

(a) consists of information relating to the physical or mental health or condition of an individual, and

(b) has been made by or on behalf of a health professional in connection with the care of that individual.

69. Meaning of 'health professional'

(1) In this Act 'health professional' means any of the following—

(a) a registered medical practitioner,

(b) a registered dentist as defined by section 53(1) of the Dentists Act 1984,

(c)   a registered optician as defined by section 36(1) of the Opticians Act 1989,

(d)   a registered pharmaceutical chemist as defined by section 24(1) of the Pharmacy Act 1954 or a registered person as defined by Article 2(2) of the Pharmacy (Northern Ireland) Order 1976,

(e)   a registered nurse, midwife or health visitor,

(f)   a registered osteopath as defined by section 41 of the Osteopaths Act 1993,

(g)   a registered chiropractor as defined by section 43 of the Chiropractors Act 1994,

(h)   any person who is registered as a member of a profession to which the Professions Supplementary to Medicine Act 1960 for the time being extends,

(i)   a clinical psychologist, child psychotherapist or speech therapist,

(j)   a music therapist employed by a health service body, and

(k)   a scientist employed by such a body as head of a department.

(2)   In subsection (1)(a) 'registered medical practitioner' includes any person who is provisionally registered under section 15 or 21 of the Medical Act 1983 and is engaged in such employment as is mentioned in subsection (3) of that section.

(3)   In subsection (1) 'health service body' means—

(a)   a Health Authority established under section 8 of the National Health Service Act 1977,

(b)   a Special Health Authority established under section 11 of that Act,

(c)   a Health Board within the meaning of the National Health Service (Scotland) Act 1978,

(d)   a Special Health Board within the meaning of that Act,

(e)   the managers of a State Hospital provided under section 102 of that Act,

(f)   a National Health Service trust first established under section 5 of the National Health Service and Community Care Act 1990 or section 12A of the National Health Service (Scotland) Act 1978,

(g)   a Health and Social Services Board established under Article 16 of the Health and Personal Social Services (Northern Ireland) Order 1972,

(h)   a special health and social services agency established under the Health and Personal Social Services (Special Agencies) (Northern Ireland) Order 1990, or

(i)   a Health and Social Services trust established under Article 10 of the Health and Personal Social Services (Northern Ireland) Order 1991.

70.   Supplementary definitions

(1)   In this Act, unless the context otherwise requires—

'business' includes any trade or profession;

'the Commissioner' means the Data Protection Commissioner;

'credit reference agency' has the same meaning as in the Consumer Credit Act 1974;

'the Data Protection Directive' means Directive 95/46/EC on the protection of individuals with regard to the processing of personal data and on the free movement of such data;

'EEA State' means a State which is a contracting party to the Agreement on the European Economic Area signed at Oporto on 2nd May 1992 as adjusted by the Protocol signed at Brussels on 17th March 1993;

'enactment' includes an enactment passed after this Act;

'government department' includes a Northern Ireland department and any body or authority exercising statutory functions on behalf of the Crown;

'Minister of the Crown' has the same meaning as in the Ministers of the Crown Act 1975;

'public register' means any register which pursuant to a requirement imposed—

    (a)   by or under any enactment, or

    (b)   in pursuance of any international agreement,

is open to public inspection or open to inspection by any person having a legitimate interest;

'pupil'—

    (a)   in relation to a school in England and Wales, means a registered pupil within the meaning of the Education Act 1996,

    (b)   in relation to a school in Scotland, means a pupil within the meaning of the Education (Scotland) Act 1980, and

    (c)   in relation to a school in Northern Ireland, means a registered pupil within the meaning of the Education and Libraries (Northern Ireland) Order 1986;

'recipient', in relation to any personal data, means any person to whom the data are disclosed, including any person (such as an employee or agent of the data controller, a data processor or an employee or agent of a data processor) to whom they are disclosed in the course of processing the data for the data controller, but does not include any person to whom disclosure is or may be made as a result of, or with a view to, a particular inquiry by or on behalf of that person made in the exercise of any power conferred by law;

'registered company' means a company registered under the enactments relating to companies for the time being in force in the United Kingdom;

'school'—

    (a)   in relation to England and Wales, has the same meaning as in the Education Act 1996,

    (b)   in relation to Scotland, has the same meaning as in the Education (Scotland) Act 1980, and

    (c)   in relation to Northern Ireland, has the same meaning as in the Education and Libraries (Northern Ireland) Order 1986;

'teacher' includes—

    (a)   in Great Britain, head teacher, and

    (b)   in Northern Ireland, the principal of a school;

'third party', in relation to personal data, means any person other than—

    (a)   the data subject,

    (b)   the data controller, or

    (c)   any data processor or other person authorised to process data for the data controller or processor;

'the Tribunal' means the Data Protection Tribunal.

(2)   For the purposes of this Act data are inaccurate if they are incorrect or misleading as to any matter of fact.

71. Index of defined expressions

The following Table shows provisions defining or otherwise explaining expressions used in this Act (other than provisions defining or explaining an expression only used in the same section or Schedule)—

accessible record	section 68
address (in Part III)	section 16(3)
business	section 70(1)
the Commissioner	section 70(1)
credit reference agency	section 70(1)
data	section 1(1)
data controller	sections 1(1) and (4) and 63(3)
data processor	section 1(1)
the Data Protection Directive	section 70(1)
data protection principles	section 4 and Schedule 1
data subject	section 1(1)
disclosing (of personal data)	section 1(2)(b)
EEA State	section 70(1)
enactment	section 70(1)
enforcement notice	section 40(1)
fees regulations (in Part III)	section 16(2)
government department	section 70(1)
health professional	section 69
inaccurate (in relation to data)	section 70(2)
information notice	section 43(1)
Minister of the Crown	section 70(1)
the non-disclosure provisions (in Part IV)	section 27(3)
notification regulations (in Part III)	section 16(2)
obtaining (of personal data)	section 1(2)(a)
personal data	section 1(1)
prescribed (in Part III)	section 16(2)
processing (of information or data)	section 1(1) and paragraph 5 of Schedule 8
public register	section 70(1)
publish (in relation to journalistic, literary or artistic material)	section 32(6)
pupil (in relation to a school)	section 70(1)
recipient (in relation to personal data)	section 70(1)
recording (of personal data)	section 1(2)(a)
registered company	section 70(1)
registrable particulars (in Part III)	section 16(1)
relevant filing system	section 1(1)
school	section 70(1)
sensitive personal data	section 2
special information notice	section 44(1)
the special purposes	section 3
the subject information provisions (in Part IV)	section 27(2)
teacher	section 70(1)
third party (in relation to processing of personal data)	section 70(1)
the Tribunal	section 70(1)
using (of personal data)	section 1(2)(b).

72. Modifications of Act

During the period beginning with the commencement of this section and ending with 23rd October 2007, the provisions of this Act shall have effect subject to the modifications set out in Schedule 13.

73. Transitional provisions and savings

Schedule 14 (which contains transitional provisions and savings) has effect.

74. Minor and consequential amendments and repeals and revocations

(1) Schedule 15 (which contains minor and consequential amendments) has effect.

(2) The enactments and instruments specified in Schedule 16 are repealed or revoked to the extent specified.

75. Short title, commencement and extent

(1) This Act may be cited as the Data Protection Act 1998.

(2) The following provisions of this Act—

(a) sections 1 to 3,

(b) section 25(1) and (4),

(c) section 26,

(d) sections 67 to 71,

(e) this section,

(f) paragraph 17 of Schedule 5,

(g) Schedule 11,

(h) Schedule 12, and

(i) so much of any other provision of this Act as confers any power to make subordinate legislation,

shall come into force on the day on which this Act is passed.

(3) The remaining provisions of this Act shall come into force on such day as the Secretary of State may by order appoint; and different days may be appointed for different purposes.

(4) The day appointed under subsection (3) for the coming into force of section 56 must not be earlier than the first day on which sections 112, 113 and 115 of the Police Act 1997 (which provide for the issue by the Secretary of State of criminal conviction certificates, criminal record certificates and enhanced criminal record certificates) are all in force.

(5) Subject to subsection (6), this Act extends to Northern Ireland.

(6) Any amendment, repeal or revocation made by Schedule 15 or 16 has the same extent as that of the enactment or instrument to which it relates.

SCHEDULES

Section 4(1) and (2)   SCHEDULE 1
THE DATA PROTECTION PRINCIPLES

PART I
THE PRINCIPLES

1. Personal data shall be processed fairly and lawfully and, in particular, shall not be processed unless—

(a) at least one of the conditions in Schedule 2 is met, and

(b)   in the case of sensitive personal data, at least one of the conditions in Schedule 3 is also met.

2.   Personal data shall be obtained only for one or more specified and lawful purposes, and shall not be further processed in any manner incompatible with that purpose or those purposes.

3.   Personal data shall be adequate, relevant and not excessive in relation to the purpose or purposes for which they are processed.

4.   Personal data shall be accurate and, where necessary, kept up to date.

5.   Personal data processed for any purpose or purposes shall not be kept for longer than is necessary for that purpose or those purposes.

6.   Personal data shall be processed in accordance with the rights of data subjects under this Act.

7.   Appropriate technical and organisational measures shall be taken against unauthorised or unlawful processing of personal data and against accidental loss or destruction of, or damage to, personal data.

8.   Personal data shall not be transferred to a country or territory outside the European Economic Area unless that country or territory ensures an adequate level of protection for the rights and freedoms of data subjects in relation to the processing of personal data.

PART II
INTERPRETATION OF THE PRINCIPLES IN PART I

The first principle

1.—(1)   In determining for the purposes of the first principle whether personal data are processed fairly, regard is to be had to the method by which they are obtained, including in particular whether any person from whom they are obtained is deceived or misled as to the purpose or purposes for which they are to be processed.

(2)   Subject to paragraph 2, for the purposes of the first principle data are to be treated as obtained fairly if they consist of information obtained from a person who—

(a)   is authorised by or under any enactment to supply it, or

(b)   is required to supply it by or under any enactment or by any convention or other instrument imposing an international obligation on the United Kingdom.

2.—(1)   Subject to paragraph 3, for the purposes of the first principle personal data are not to be treated as processed fairly unless—

(a)   in the case of data obtained from the data subject, the data controller ensures so far as practicable that the data subject has, is provided with, or has made readily available to him, the information specified in subparagraph (3), and

(b)   in any other case, the data controller ensures so far as practicable that, before the relevant time or as soon as practicable after that time, the data subject has, is provided with, or has made readily available to him, the information specified in sub-paragraph (3).

(2)   In sub-paragraph (1)(b) 'the relevant time' means—

(a)   the time when the data controller first processes the data, or

(b)   in a case where at that time disclosure to a third party within a reasonable period is envisaged—

(i)   if the data are in fact disclosed to such a person within that period, the time when the data are first disclosed,

(ii)   if within that period the data controller becomes, or ought to become, aware that the data are unlikely to be disclosed to such a person within that period, the time when the data controller does become, or ought to become, so aware, or

(iii)   in any other case, the end of that period.

(3)   The information referred to in sub-paragraph (1) is as follows, namely—

(a)   the identity of the data controller,

(b)   if he has nominated a representative for the purposes of this Act, the identity of that representative,

(c)   the purpose or purposes for which the data are intended to be processed, and

(d)   any further information which is necessary, having regard to the specific circumstances in which the data are or are to be processed, to enable processing in respect of the data subject to be fair.

3.—(1)   Paragraph 2(1)(b) does not apply where either of the primary conditions in sub-paragraph (2), together with such further conditions as may be prescribed by the Secretary of State by order, are met.

(2)   The primary conditions referred to in sub-paragraph (1) are—

(a)   that the provision of that information would involve a disproportionate effort, or

(b)   that the recording of the information to be contained in the data by, or the disclosure of the data by, the data controller is necessary for compliance with any legal obligation to which the data controller is subject, other than an obligation imposed by contract.

4.—(1)   Personal data which contain a general identifier falling within a description prescribed by the Secretary of State by order are not to be treated as processed fairly and lawfully unless they are processed in compliance with any conditions so prescribed in relation to general identifiers of that description.

(2)   In sub-paragraph (1) 'a general identifier' means any identifier (such as, for example, a number or code used for identification purposes) which—

(a)   relates to an individual, and

(b)   forms part of a set of similar identifiers which is of general application.

The second principle

5.   The purpose or purposes for which personal data are obtained may in particular be specified—

(a)   in a notice given for the purposes of paragraph 2 by the data controller to the data subject, or

(b)   in a notification given to the Commissioner under Part III of this Act.

6.   In determining whether any disclosure of personal data is compatible with the purpose or purposes for which the data were obtained, regard is to be had to the purpose or purposes for which the personal data are intended to be processed by any person to whom they are disclosed.

The fourth principle

7.   The fourth principle is not to be regarded as being contravened by reason of any inaccuracy in personal data which accurately record information obtained by the data controller from the data subject or a third party in a case where—

(a)   having regard to the purpose or purposes for which the data were obtained and further processed, the data controller has taken reasonable steps to ensure the accuracy of the data, and

(b)   if the data subject has notified the data controller of the data subject's view that the data are inaccurate, the data indicate that fact.

The sixth principle

8.   A person is to be regarded as contravening the sixth principle if, but only if—

(a)   he contravenes section 7 by failing to supply information in accordance with that section,

(b)   he contravenes section 10 by failing to comply with a notice given under subsection (1) of that section to the extent that the notice is justified or by failing to give a notice under subsection (3) of that section,

(c)   he contravenes section 11 by failing to comply with a notice given under subsection (1) of that section, or

(d)   he contravenes section 12 by failing to comply with a notice given under subsection (1) or (2)(b) of that section or by failing to give a notification under subsection (2)(a) of that section or a notice under subsection (3) of that section.

The seventh principle

9.   Having regard to the state of technological development and the cost of implementing any measures, the measures must ensure a level of security appropriate to—

(a)   the harm that might result from such unauthorised or unlawful processing or accidental loss, destruction or damage as are mentioned in the seventh principle, and

(b)   the nature of the data to be protected.

10.   The data controller must take reasonable steps to ensure the reliability of any employees of his who have access to the personal data.

11.   Where processing of personal data is carried out by a data processor on behalf of a data controller, the data controller must in order to comply with the seventh principle—

(a)   choose a data processor providing sufficient guarantees in respect of the technical and organisational security measures governing the processing to be carried out, and

(b)   take reasonable steps to ensure compliance with those measures.

12.   Where processing of personal data is carried out by a data processor on behalf of a data controller, the data controller is not to be regarded as complying with the seventh principle unless—

(a)   the processing is carried out under a contract—

(i)   which is made or evidenced in writing, and

(ii)   under which the data processor is to act only on instructions from the data controller, and

(b)   the contract requires the data processor to comply with obligations equivalent to those imposed on a data controller by the seventh principle.

The eighth principle

13.   An adequate level of protection is one which is adequate in all the circumstances of the case, having regard in particular to—

(a)   the nature of the personal data,

(b)   the country or territory of origin of the information contained in the data,

(c)   the country or territory of final destination of that information,

(d)   the purposes for which and period during which the data are intended to be processed,

(e)   the law in force in the country or territory in question,

(f)   the international obligations of that country or territory,

(g)   any relevant codes of conduct or other rules which are enforceable in that country or territory (whether generally or by arrangement in particular cases), and

(h)   any security measures taken in respect of the data in that country or territory.

14.   The eighth principle does not apply to a transfer falling within any paragraph of Schedule 4, except in such circumstances and to such extent as the Secretary of State may by order provide.

15.—(1)   Where—

(a)   in any proceedings under this Act any question arises as to whether the requirement of the eighth principle as to an adequate level of protection is met in relation to the transfer of any personal data to a country or territory outside the European Economic Area, and

(b)   a Community finding has been made in relation to transfers of the kind in question,

that question is to be determined in accordance with that finding.

(2)   In sub-paragraph (1) 'Community finding' means a finding of the European Commission, under the procedure provided for in Article 31(2) of the Data Protection Directive, that a country or territory outside the European Economic Area does, or does not, ensure an adequate level of protection within the meaning of Article 25(2) of the Directive.

Section 4(3)   SCHEDULE 2
CONDITIONS RELEVANT FOR PURPOSES OF THE FIRST PRINCIPLE:
PROCESSING OF ANY PERSONAL DATA

1.   The data subject has given his consent to the processing.

2.   The processing is necessary—

(a)   for the performance of a contract to which the data subject is a party, or

(b)   for the taking of steps at the request of the data subject with a view to entering into a contract.

3.   The processing is necessary for compliance with any legal obligation to which the data controller is subject, other than an obligation imposed by contract.

4.   The processing is necessary in order to protect the vital interests of the data subject.

5.   The processing is necessary—

(a)   for the administration of justice,

(b)   for the exercise of any functions conferred on any person by or under any enactment,

(c)   for the exercise of any functions of the Crown, a Minister of the Crown or a government department, or

(d)   for the exercise of any other functions of a public nature exercised in the public interest by any person.

6.—(1)   The processing is necessary for the purposes of legitimate interests pursued by the data controller or by the third party or parties to whom the data are disclosed, except where the processing is unwarranted in any particular case by reason of prejudice to the rights and freedoms or legitimate interests of the data subject.

(2)   The Secretary of State may by order specify particular circumstances in which this condition is, or is not, to be taken to be satisfied.

Section 4(3)   SCHEDULE 3
CONDITIONS RELEVANT FOR PURPOSES OF THE FIRST PRINCIPLE:
PROCESSING OF SENSITIVE PERSONAL DATA

1.   The data subject has given his explicit consent to the processing of the personal data.

2.—(1)   The processing is necessary for the purposes of exercising or performing any right or obligation which is conferred or imposed by law on the data controller in connection with employment.

(2)   The Secretary of State may by order—

(a)   exclude the application of sub-paragraph (1) in such cases as may be specified, or

(b)   provide that, in such cases as may be specified, the condition in sub-paragraph (1) is not to be regarded as satisfied unless such further conditions as may be specified in the order are also satisfied.

3.   The processing is necessary—

(a)   in order to protect the vital interests of the data subject or another person, in a case where—

(i)   consent cannot be given by or on behalf of the data subject, or

(ii)   the data controller cannot reasonably be expected to obtain the consent of the data subject, or

(b)   in order to protect the vital interests of another person, in a case where consent by or on behalf of the data subject has been unreasonably withheld.

4.   The processing—

(a)   is carried out in the course of its legitimate activities by any body or association which—

(i)   is not established or conducted for profit, and

(ii)   exists for political, philosophical, religious or trade-union purposes,

(b)   is carried out with appropriate safeguards for the rights and freedoms of data subjects,

(c)   relates only to individuals who either are members of the body or association or have regular contact with it in connection with its purposes, and

(d)   does not involve disclosure of the personal data to a third party without the consent of the data subject.

5.   The information contained in the personal data has been made public as a result of steps deliberately taken by the data subject.

6.   The processing—

(a) is necessary for the purpose of, or in connection with, any legal proceedings (including prospective legal proceedings),

(b) is necessary for the purpose of obtaining legal advice, or

(c) is otherwise necessary for the purposes of establishing, exercising or defending legal rights.

7.—(1) The processing is necessary—

(a) for the administration of justice,

(b) for the exercise of any functions conferred on any person by or under an enactment, or

(c) for the exercise of any functions of the Crown, a Minister of the Crown or a government department.

(2) The Secretary of State may by order—

(a) exclude the application of sub-paragraph (1) in such cases as may be specified, or

(b) provide that, in such cases as may be specified, the condition in sub-paragraph (1) is not to be regarded as satisfied unless such further conditions as may be specified in the order are also satisfied.

8.—(1) The processing is necessary for medical purposes and is undertaken by—

(a) a health professional, or

(b) a person who in the circumstances owes a duty of confidentiality which is equivalent to that which would arise if that person were a health professional.

(2) In this paragraph 'medical purposes' includes the purposes of preventative medicine, medical diagnosis, medical research, the provision of care and treatment and the management of healthcare services.

9.—(1) The processing—

(a) is of sensitive personal data consisting of information as to racial or ethnic origin,

(b) is necessary for the purpose of identifying or keeping under review the existence or absence of equality of opportunity or treatment between persons of different racial or ethnic origins, with a view to enabling such equality to be promoted or maintained, and

(c) is carried out with appropriate safeguards for the rights and freedoms of data subjects.

(2) The Secretary of State may by order specify circumstances in which processing falling within sub-paragraph (1)(a) and (b) is, or is not, to be taken for the purposes of sub-paragraph (1)(c) to be carried out with appropriate safeguards for the rights and freedoms of data subjects.

10. The personal data are processed in circumstances specified in an order made by the Secretary of State for the purposes of this paragraph.

Section 4(3)   **SCHEDULE 4**
CASES WHERE THE EIGHTH PRINCIPLE DOES NOT APPLY

1. The data subject has given his consent to the transfer.

2. The transfer is necessary—

(a) for the performance of a contract between the data subject and the data controller, or

(b) for the taking of steps at the request of the data subject with a view to his entering into a contract with the data controller.

3. The transfer is necessary—

   (a) for the conclusion of a contract between the data controller and a person other than the data subject which—

      (i)   is entered into at the request of the data subject, or

      (ii)   is in the interests of the data subject, or

   (b) for the performance of such a contract.

4.—(1) The transfer is necessary for reasons of substantial public interest.

(2) The Secretary of State may by order specify—

   (a) circumstances in which a transfer is to be taken for the purposes of sub-paragraph (1) to be necessary for reasons of substantial public interest, and

   (b) circumstances in which a transfer which is not required by or under an enactment is not to be taken for the purpose of sub-paragraph (1) to be necessary for reasons of substantial public interest.

5. The transfer—

   (a) is necessary for the purpose of, or in connection with, any legal proceedings (including prospective legal proceedings),

   (b) is necessary for the purpose of obtaining legal advice, or

   (c) is otherwise necessary for the purposes of establishing, exercising or defending legal rights.

6. The transfer is necessary in order to protect the vital interests of the data subject.

7. The transfer is of part of the personal data on a public register and any conditions subject to which the register is open to inspection are complied with by any person to whom the data are or may be disclosed after the transfer.

8. The transfer is made on terms which are of a kind approved by the Commissioner as ensuring adequate safeguards for the rights and freedoms of data subjects.

9. The transfer has been authorised by the Commissioner as being made in such a manner as to ensure adequate safeguards for the rights and freedoms of data subjects.

Section 6(7)   SCHEDULE 5
THE DATA PROTECTION COMMISSIONER AND THE DATA PROTECTION TRIBUNAL

PART I
THE COMMISSIONER

Status and capacity

1.—(1) The corporation sole by the name of the Data Protection Registrar established by the Data Protection Act 1984 shall continue in existence by the name of the Data Protection Commissioner.

(2) The Commissioner and his officers and staff are not to be regarded as servants or agents of the Crown.

Tenure of office

2.—(1) Subject to the provisions of this paragraph, the Commissioner shall hold office for such term not exceeding five years as may be determined at the time of his appointment.

(2)   The Commissioner may be relieved of his office by Her Majesty at his own request.

(3)   The Commissioner may be removed from office by Her Majesty in pursuance of an Address from both Houses of Parliament.

(4)   The Commissioner shall in any case vacate his office—

(a)   on completing the year of service in which he attains the age of sixty-five years, or

(b)   if earlier, on completing his fifteenth year of service.

(5)   Subject to sub-paragraph (4), a person who ceases to be Commissioner on the expiration of his term of office shall be eligible for re-appointment, but a person may not be re-appointed for a third or subsequent term as Commissioner unless, by reason of special circumstances, the person's re-appointment for such a term is desirable in the public interest.

Salary etc.

3.—(1)   There shall be paid—

(a)   to the Commissioner such salary, and

(b)   to or in respect of the Commissioner such pension,

as may be specified by a resolution of the House of Commons.

(2)   A resolution for the purposes of this paragraph may—

(a)   specify the salary or pension,

(b)   provide that the salary or pension is to be the same as, or calculated on the same basis as, that payable to, or to or in respect of, a person employed in a specified office under, or in a specified capacity in the service of, the Crown, or

(c)   specify the salary or pension and provide for it to be increased by reference to such variables as may be specified in the resolution.

(3)   A resolution for the purposes of this paragraph may take effect from the date on which it is passed or from any earlier or later date specified in the resolution.

(4)   A resolution for the purposes of this paragraph may make different provision in relation to the pension payable to or in respect of different holders of the office of Commissioner.

(5)   Any salary or pension payable under this paragraph shall be charged on and issued out of the Consolidated Fund.

(6)   In this paragraph 'pension' includes an allowance or gratuity and any reference to the payment of a pension includes a reference to the making of payments towards the provision of a pension.

Officers and staff

4.—(1)   The Commissioner—

(a)   shall appoint a deputy commissioner, and

(b)   may appoint such number of other officers and staff as he may determine.

(2)   The remuneration and other conditions of service of the persons appointed under this paragraph shall be determined by the Commissioner.

(3)   The Commissioner may pay such pensions, allowances or gratuities to or in respect of the persons appointed under this paragraph, or make such payments towards the provision of such pensions, allowances or gratuities, as he may determine.

(4) The references in sub-paragraph (3) to pensions, allowances or gratuities to or in respect of the persons appointed under this paragraph include references to pensions, allowances or gratuities by way of compensation to or in respect of any of those persons who suffer loss of office or employment.

(5) Any determination under sub-paragraph (1)(b), (2) or (3) shall require the approval of the Secretary of State.

(6) The Employers' Liability (Compulsory Insurance) Act 1969 shall not require insurance to be effected by the Commissioner.

5.—(1) The deputy commissioner shall perform the functions conferred by this Act on the Commissioner during any vacancy in that office or at any time when the Commissioner is for any reason unable to act.

(2) Without prejudice to sub-paragraph (1), any functions of the Commissioner under this Act may, to the extent authorised by him, be performed by any of his officers or staff.

Authentication of seal of the Commissioner

6. The application of the seal of the Commissioner shall be authenticated by his signature or by the signature of some other person authorised for the purpose.

Presumption of authenticity of documents issued by the Commissioner

7. Any document purporting to be an instrument issued by the Commissioner and to be duly executed under the Commissioner's seal or to be signed by or on behalf of the Commissioner shall be received in evidence and shall be deemed to be such an instrument unless the contrary is shown.

Money

8. The Secretary of State may make payments to the Commissioner out of money provided by Parliament.

9.—(1) All fees and other sums received by the Commissioner in the exercise of his functions under this Act or section 159 of the Consumer Credit Act 1974 shall be paid by him to the Secretary of State.

(2) Sub-paragraph (1) shall not apply where the Secretary of State, with the consent of the Treasury, otherwise directs.

(3) Any sums received by the Secretary of State under sub-paragraph (1) shall be paid into the Consolidated Fund.

Accounts

10.—(1) It shall be the duty of the Commissioner—

    (a) to keep proper accounts and other records in relation to the accounts,

    (b) to prepare in respect of each financial year a statement of account in such form as the Secretary of State may direct, and

    (c) to send copies of that statement to the Comptroller and Auditor General on or before 31st August next following the end of the year to which the statement relates or on or before such earlier date after the end of that year as the Treasury may direct.

(2) The Comptroller and Auditor General shall examine and certify any statement sent to him under this paragraph and lay copies of it together with his report thereon before each House of Parliament.

(3)   In this paragraph 'financial year' means a period of twelve months beginning with 1st April.

Application of Part I in Scotland

11.   Paragraphs 1(1), 6 and 7 do not extend to Scotland.

PART II
THE TRIBUNAL

Tenure of office

12.—(1)   Subject to the following provisions of this paragraph, a member of the Tribunal shall hold and vacate his office in accordance with the terms of his appointment and shall, on ceasing to hold office, be eligible for re-appointment.

(2)   Any member of the Tribunal may at any time resign his office by notice in writing to the Lord Chancellor (in the case of the chairman or a deputy chairman) or to the Secretary of State (in the case of any other member).

(3)   A person who is the chairman or deputy chairman of the Tribunal shall vacate his office on the day on which he attains the age of seventy years; but this sub-paragraph is subject to section 26(4) to (6) of the Judicial Pensions and Retirement Act 1993 (power to authorise continuance in office up to the age of seventy-five years).

Salary etc.

13.   The Secretary of State shall pay to the members of the Tribunal out of money provided by Parliament such remuneration and allowances as he may determine.

Officers and staff

14.   The Secretary of State may provide the Tribunal with such officers and staff as he thinks necessary for the proper discharge of its functions.

Expenses

15.   Such expenses of the Tribunal as the Secretary of State may determine shall be defrayed by the Secretary of State out of money provided by Parliament.

PART III
TRANSITIONAL PROVISIONS

16.   Any reference in any enactment, instrument or other document to the Data Protection Registrar shall be construed, in relation to any time after the commencement of section 6(1), as a reference to the Commissioner.

17.   Any reference in this Act or in any instrument under this Act to the Commissioner shall be construed, in relation to any time before the commencement of section 6(1), as a reference to the Data Protection Registrar.

Sections 28(12), 48(5)   SCHEDULE 6
APPEAL PROCEEDINGS

Hearing of appeals

1.   For the purpose of hearing and determining appeals or any matter preliminary or incidental to an appeal the Tribunal shall sit at such times and in such places as the chairman or a deputy chairman may direct and may sit in two or more divisions.

Constitution of Tribunal in national security cases

2.—(1) The Lord Chancellor shall from time to time designate, from among the chairman and deputy chairmen appointed by him under section 6(4)(a) and (b), those persons who are to be capable of hearing appeals under section 28(4) or (6).

(2) A designation under sub-paragraph (1) may at any time be revoked by the Lord Chancellor.

3. In any case where the application of paragraph 6(1) is excluded by rules under paragraph 7, the Tribunal shall be duly constituted for an appeal under section 28(4) or (6) if it consists of three of the persons designated under paragraph 2(1), of whom one shall be designated by the Lord Chancellor to preside.

Constitution of Tribunal in other cases

4.—(1) Subject to any rules made under paragraph 7, the Tribunal shall be duly constituted for an appeal under section 48(1), (2) or (4) if it consists of—

(a) the chairman or a deputy chairman (who shall preside), and

(b) an equal number of the members appointed respectively in accordance with paragraphs (a) and (b) of section 6(6).

(2) The members who are to constitute the Tribunal in accordance with subparagraph (1) shall be nominated by the chairman or, if he is for any reason unable to act, by a deputy chairman.

Determination of questions by full Tribunal

5. The determination of any question before the Tribunal when constituted in accordance with paragraph 3 or 4 shall be according to the opinion of the majority of the members hearing the appeal.

Ex parte proceedings

6.—(1) Subject to any rules made under paragraph 7, the jurisdiction of the Tribunal in respect of an appeal under section 28(4) or (6) shall be exercised ex parte by one or more persons designated under paragraph 2(1).

(2) Subject to any rules made under paragraph 7, the jurisdiction of the Tribunal in respect of an appeal under section 48(3) shall be exercised ex parte by the chairman or a deputy chairman sitting alone.

Rules of procedure

7.—(1) The Secretary of State may make rules for regulating the exercise of the rights of appeal conferred by sections 28(4) or (6) and 48 and the practice and procedure of the Tribunal.

(2) Rules under this paragraph may in particular make provision—

(a) with respect to the period within which an appeal can be brought and the burden of proof on an appeal,

(b) for the summoning (or, in Scotland, citation) of witnesses and the administration of oaths,

(c) for securing the production of documents and material used for the processing of personal data,

(d) for the inspection, examination, operation and testing of any equipment or material used in connection with the processing of personal data,

(e)   for the hearing of an appeal wholly or partly in camera,

(f)   for hearing an appeal in the absence of the appellant or for determining an appeal without a hearing,

(g)   for enabling an appeal under section 48(1) against an information notice to be determined by the chairman or a deputy chairman,

(h)   for enabling any matter preliminary or incidental to an appeal to be dealt with by the chairman or a deputy chairman,

(i)   for the awarding of costs or, in Scotland, expenses,

(j)   for the publication of reports of the Tribunal's decisions, and

(k)   for conferring on the Tribunal such ancillary powers as the Secretary of State thinks necessary for the proper discharge of its functions.

(3)   In making rules under this paragraph which relate to appeals under section 28(4) or (6) the Secretary of State shall have regard, in particular, to the need to secure that information is not disclosed contrary to the public interest.

Obstruction etc.

8.—(1)   If any person is guilty of any act or omission in relation to proceedings before the Tribunal which, if those proceedings were proceedings before a court having power to commit for contempt, would constitute contempt of court, the Tribunal may certify the offence to the High Court or, in Scotland, the Court of Session.

(2)   Where an offence is so certified, the court may inquire into the matter and, after hearing any witness who may be produced against or on behalf of the person charged with the offence, and after hearing any statement that may be offered in defence, deal with him in any manner in which it could deal with him if he had committed the like offence in relation to the court.

Section 37   SCHEDULE 7
                    MISCELLANEOUS EXEMPTIONS

Confidential references given by the data controller

1.   Personal data are exempt from section 7 if they consist of a reference given or to be given in confidence by the data controller for the purposes of—

(a)   the education, training or employment, or prospective education, training or employment, of the data subject,

(b)   the appointment, or prospective appointment, of the data subject to any office, or

(c)   the provision, or prospective provision, by the data subject of any service.

Armed forces

2.   Personal data are exempt from the subject information provisions in any case to the extent to which the application of those provisions would be likely to prejudice the combat effectiveness of any of the armed forces of the Crown.

Judicial appointments and honours

3.   Personal data processed for the purposes of—

(a)   assessing any person's suitability for judicial office or the office of Queen's Counsel, or

(b)   the conferring by the Crown of any honour,
are exempt from the subject information provisions.

Crown employment and Crown or Ministerial appointments

4.   The Secretary of State may by order exempt from the subject information provisions personal data processed for the purposes of assessing any person's suitability for—

(a)   employment by or under the Crown, or

(b)   any office to which appointments are made by Her Majesty, by a Minister of the Crown or by a Northern Ireland department.

Management forecasts etc.

5.   Personal data processed for the purposes of management forecasting or management planning to assist the data controller in the conduct of any business or other activity are exempt from the subject information provisions in any case to the extent to which the application of those provisions would be likely to prejudice the conduct of that business or other activity.

Corporate finance

6.—(1)   Where personal data are processed for the purposes of, or in connection with, a corporate finance service provided by a relevant person—

(a)   the data are exempt from the subject information provisions in any case to the extent to which either—

(i)   the application of those provisions to the data could affect the price of any instrument which is already in existence or is to be or may be created, or

(ii)   the data controller reasonably believes that the application of those provisions to the data could affect the price of any such instrument, and

(b)   to the extent that the data are not exempt from the subject information provisions by virtue of paragraph (a), they are exempt from those provisions if the exemption is required for the purpose of safeguarding an important economic or financial interest of the United Kingdom.

(2)   For the purposes of sub-paragraph (1)(b) the Secretary of State may by order specify—

(a)   matters to be taken into account in determining whether exemption from the subject information provisions is required for the purpose of safeguarding an important economic or financial interest of the United Kingdom, or

(b)   circumstances in which exemption from those provisions is, or is not, to be taken to be required for that purpose.

(3)   In this paragraph—

'corporate finance service' means a service consisting in—

(a)   underwriting in respect of issues of, or the placing of issues of, any instrument,

(b)   advice to undertakings on capital structure, industrial strategy and related matters and advice and service relating to mergers and the purchase of undertakings, or

(c)   services relating to such underwriting as is mentioned in paragraph (a);
'instrument' means any instrument listed in section B of the Annex to the Council
Directive on investment services in the securities field (93/22/EEC), as set out in
Schedule 1 to the Investment Services Regulations 1995;
'price' includes value;
'relevant person' means—

(a)   any person who is authorised under Chapter III of Part I of the Financial
Services Act 1986 or is an exempted person under Chapter IV of Part I of that Act,

(b)   any person who, but for Part III or IV of Schedule 1 to that Act, would
require authorisation under that Act,

(c)   any European investment firm within the meaning given by Regulation 3
of the Investment Services Regulations 1995,

(d)   any person who, in the course of his employment, provides to his
employer a service falling within paragraph (b) or (c) of the definition of 'corporate
finance service', or

(e)   any partner who provides to other partners in the partnership a service
falling within either of those paragraphs.

Negotiations

7.   Personal data which consist of records of the intentions of the data controller
in relation to any negotiations with the data subject are exempt from the subject
information provisions in any case to the extent to which the application of those
provisions would be likely to prejudice those negotiations.

Examination marks

8.—(1)   Section 7 shall have effect subject to the provisions of sub-paragraphs (2)
to (4) in the case of personal data consisting of marks or other information processed
by a data controller—

(a)   for the purpose of determining the results of an academic, professional or
other examination or of enabling the results of any such examination to be
determined, or

(b)   in consequence of the determination of any such results.

(2)   Where the relevant day falls before the day on which the results of the
examination are announced, the period mentioned in section 7(8) shall be extended
until—

(a)   the end of five months beginning with the relevant day, or

(b)   the end of forty days beginning with the date of the announcement,
whichever is the earlier.

(3)   Where by virtue of sub-paragraph (2) a period longer than the prescribed
period elapses after the relevant day before the request is complied with, the
information to be supplied pursuant to the request shall be supplied both by reference
to the data in question at the time when the request is received and (if different) by
reference to the data as from time to time held in the period beginning when the
request is received and ending when it is complied with.

(4)   For the purposes of this paragraph the results of an examination shall be
treated as announced when they are first published or (if not published) when they
are first made available or communicated to the candidate in question.

(5) In this paragraph—

'examination' includes any process for determining the knowledge, intelligence, skill or ability of a candidate by reference to his performance in any test, work or other activity;

'the prescribed period' means forty days or such other period as is for the time being prescribed under section 7 in relation to the personal data in question;

'relevant day' has the same meaning as in section 7.

Examination scripts etc.

9.—(1) Personal data consisting of information recorded by candidates during an academic, professional or other examination are exempt from section 7.

(2) In this paragraph 'examination' has the same meaning as in paragraph 8.

Legal professional privilege

10. Personal data are exempt from the subject information provisions if the data consist of information in respect of which a claim to legal professional privilege or, in Scotland, to confidentiality as between client and professional legal adviser, could be maintained in legal proceedings.

Self-incrimination

11.—(1) A person need not comply with any request or order under section 7 to the extent that compliance would, by revealing evidence of the commission of any offence other than an offence under this Act, expose him to proceedings for that offence.

(2) Information disclosed by any person in compliance with any request or order under section 7 shall not be admissible against him in proceedings for an offence under this Act.

Section 39
SCHEDULE 8
TRANSITIONAL RELIEF

PART I
INTERPRETATION OF SCHEDULE

1.—(1) For the purposes of this Schedule, personal data are 'eligible data' at any time if, and to the extent that, they are at that time subject to processing which was already under way immediately before 24th October 1998.

(2) In this Schedule—

'eligible automated data' means eligible data which fall within paragraph (a) or (b) of the definition of 'data' in section 1(1);

'eligible manual data' means eligible data which are not eligible automated data;

'the first transitional period' means the period beginning with the commencement of this Schedule and ending with 23rd October 2001;

'the second transitional period' means the period beginning with 24th October 2001 and ending with 23rd October 2007.

PART II
EXEMPTIONS AVAILABLE BEFORE 24TH OCTOBER 2001

Manual data

2.—(1)   Eligible manual data, other than data forming part of an accessible record, are exempt from the data protection principles and Parts II and III of this Act during the first transitional period.

(2)   This paragraph does not apply to eligible manual data to which paragraph 4 applies.

3.—(1)   This paragraph applies to—

(a)   eligible manual data forming part of an accessible record, and

(b)   personal data which fall within paragraph (d) of the definition of 'data' in section 1(1) but which, because they are not subject to processing which was already under way immediately before 24th October 1998, are not eligible data for the purposes of this Schedule.

(2)   During the first transitional period, data to which this paragraph applies are exempt from—

(a)   the data protection principles, except the sixth principle so far as relating to sections 7 and 12A,

(b)   Part II of this Act, except—

(i)   section 7 (as it has effect subject to section 8) and section 12A, and

(ii)   section 15 so far as relating to those sections, and

(c)   Part III of this Act.

4.—(1)   This paragraph applies to eligible manual data which consist of information relevant to the financial standing of the data subject and in respect of which the data controller is a credit reference agency.

(2)   During the first transitional period, data to which this paragraph applies are exempt from—

(a)   the data protection principles, except the sixth principle so far as relating to sections 7 and 12A,

(b)   Part II of this Act, except—

(i)   section 7 (as it has effect subject to sections 8 and 9) and section 12A, and

(ii)   section 15 so far as relating to those sections, and

(c)   Part III of this Act.

Processing otherwise than by reference to the data subject

5.   During the first transitional period, for the purposes of this Act (apart from paragraph 1), eligible automated data are not to be regarded as being 'processed' unless the processing is by reference to the data subject.

Payrolls and accounts

6.—(1)   Subject to sub-paragraph (2), eligible automated data processed by a data controller for one or more of the following purposes—

(a)   calculating amounts payable by way of remuneration or pensions in respect of service in any employment or office or making payments of, or of sums deducted from, such remuneration or pensions, or

(b)   keeping accounts relating to any business or other activity carried on by the data controller or keeping records of purchases, sales or other transactions for the purpose of ensuring that the requisite payments are made by or to him in respect of those transactions or for the purpose of making financial or management forecasts to assist him in the conduct of any such business or activity,
are exempt from the data protection principles and Parts II and III of this Act during the first transitional period.

(2)   It shall be a condition of the exemption of any eligible automated data under this paragraph that the data are not processed for any other purpose, but the exemption is not lost by any processing of the eligible data for any other purpose if the data controller shows that he had taken such care to prevent it as in all the circumstances was reasonably required.

(3)   Data processed only for one or more of the purposes mentioned in sub-paragraph (1)(a) may be disclosed—

(a)   to any person, other than the data controller, by whom the remuneration or pensions in question are payable,

(b)   for the purpose of obtaining actuarial advice,

(c)   for the purpose of giving information as to the persons in any employment or office for use in medical research into the health of, or injuries suffered by, persons engaged in particular occupations or working in particular places or areas,

(d)   if the data subject (or a person acting on his behalf) has requested or consented to the disclosure of the data either generally or in the circumstances in which the disclosure in question is made, or

(e)   if the person making the disclosure has reasonable grounds for believing that the disclosure falls within paragraph (d).

(4)   Data processed for any of the purposes mentioned in sub-paragraph (1) may be disclosed—

(a)   for the purpose of audit or where the disclosure is for the purpose only of giving information about the data controller's financial affairs, or

(b)   in any case in which disclosure would be permitted by any other provision of this Part of this Act if sub-paragraph (2) were included among the non-disclosure provisions.

(5)   In this paragraph 'remuneration' includes remuneration in kind and 'pensions' includes gratuities or similar benefits.

Unincorporated members' clubs and mailing lists

7.   Eligible automated data processed by an unincorporated members' club and relating only to the members of the club are exempt from the data protection principles and Parts II and III of this Act during the first transitional period.

8.   Eligible automated data processed by a data controller only for the purposes of distributing, or recording the distribution of, articles or information to the data subjects and consisting only of their names, addresses or other particulars necessary for effecting the distribution, are exempt from the data protection principles and Parts II and III of this Act during the first transitional period.

9.   Neither paragraph 7 nor paragraph 8 applies to personal data relating to any data subject unless he has been asked by the club or data controller whether he objects to the data relating to him being processed as mentioned in that paragraph and has not objected.

10.   It shall be a condition of the exemption of any data under paragraph 7 that the data are not disclosed except as permitted by paragraph 11 and of the exemption under paragraph 8 that the data are not processed for any purpose other than that mentioned in that paragraph or as permitted by paragraph 11, but—

(a)   the exemption under paragraph 7 shall not be lost by any disclosure in breach of that condition, and

(b)   the exemption under paragraph 8 shall not be lost by any processing in breach of that condition,

if the data controller shows that he had taken such care to prevent it as in all the circumstances was reasonably required.

11.   Data to which paragraph 10 applies may be disclosed—

(a)   if the data subject (or a person acting on his behalf) has requested or consented to the disclosure of the data either generally or in the circumstances in which the disclosure in question is made,

(b)   if the person making the disclosure has reasonable grounds for believing that the disclosure falls within paragraph (a), or

(c)   in any case in which disclosure would be permitted by any other provision of this Part of this Act if paragraph 8 were included among the non-disclosure provisions.

Back-up data

12.   Eligible automated data which are processed only for the purpose of replacing other data in the event of the latter being lost, destroyed or impaired are exempt from section 7 during the first transitional period.

Exemption of all eligible automated data from certain requirements

13.—(1)   During the first transitional period, eligible automated data are exempt from the following provisions—

(a)   the first data protection principle to the extent to which it requires compliance with—

(i)   paragraph 2 of Part II of Schedule 1,

(ii)   the conditions in Schedule 2, and

(iii) the conditions in Schedule 3,

(b)   the seventh data protection principle to the extent to which it requires compliance with paragraph 12 of Part II of Schedule 1;

(c)   the eighth data protection principle,

(d)   in section 7(1), paragraphs (b), (c)(ii) and (d),

(e)   sections 10 and 11,

(f)   section 12, and

(g)   section 13, except so far as relating to—

(i)   any contravention of the fourth data protection principle,

(ii)   any disclosure without the consent of the data controller,

(iii) loss or destruction of data without the consent of the data controller, or

(iv)   processing for the special purposes.

(2)   The specific exemptions conferred by sub-paragraph (1)(a), (c) and (e) do not limit the data controller's general duty under the first data protection principle to ensure that processing is fair.

PART III
EXEMPTIONS AVAILABLE AFTER 23RD OCTOBER 2001 BUT BEFORE 24TH OCTOBER 2007

14.—(1)   This paragraph applies to—

(a)   eligible manual data which were held immediately before 24th October 1998, and

(b)   personal data which fall within paragraph (d) of the definition of 'data' in section 1(1) but do not fall within paragraph (a) of this sub-paragraph,

but does not apply to eligible manual data to which the exemption in paragraph 16 applies.

(2)   During the second transitional period, data to which this paragraph applies are exempt from the following provisions—

(a)   the first data protection principle except to the extent to which it requires compliance with paragraph 2 of Part II of Schedule 1,

(b)   the second, third, fourth and fifth data protection principles, and

(c)   section 14(1) to (3).

PART IV
EXEMPTIONS AFTER 23RD OCTOBER 2001 FOR HISTORICAL RESEARCH

15.   In this Part of this Schedule 'the relevant conditions' has the same meaning as in section 33.

16.—(1)   Eligible manual data which are processed only for the purpose of historical research in compliance with the relevant conditions are exempt from the provisions specified in sub-paragraph (2) after 23rd October 2001.

(2)   The provisions referred to in sub-paragraph (1) are—

(a)   the first data protection principle except in so far as it requires compliance with paragraph 2 of Part II of Schedule 1,

(b)   the second, third, fourth and fifth data protection principles, and

(c)   section 14(1) to (3).

17.—(1)   After 23rd October 2001 eligible automated data which are processed only for the purpose of historical research in compliance with the relevant conditions are exempt from the first data protection principle to the extent to which it requires compliance with the conditions in Schedules 2 and 3.

(2)   Eligible automated data which are processed—

(a)   only for the purpose of historical research,

(b)   in compliance with the relevant conditions, and

(c)   otherwise than by reference to the data subject,

are also exempt from the provisions referred to in sub-paragraph (3) after 23rd October 2001.

(3)   The provisions referred to in sub-paragraph (2) are—

(a)   the first data protection principle except in so far as it requires compliance with paragraph 2 of Part II of Schedule 1,

(b)   the second, third, fourth and fifth data protection principles, and

(c)   section 14(1) to (3).

18. For the purposes of this Part of this Schedule personal data are not to be treated as processed otherwise than for the purpose of historical research merely because the data are disclosed—

(a)   to any person, for the purpose of historical research only,

(b)   to the data subject or a person acting on his behalf,

(c)   at the request, or with the consent, of the data subject or a person acting on his behalf, or

(d)   in circumstances in which the person making the disclosure has reasonable grounds for believing that the disclosure falls within paragraph (a), (b) or (c).

PART V
EXEMPTION FROM SECTION 22

19.   Processing which was already under way immediately before 24th October 1998 is not assessable processing for the purposes of section 22.

Section 50   SCHEDULE 9
                              POWERS OF ENTRY AND INSPECTION

Issue of warrants

1.—(1) If a circuit judge is satisfied by information on oath supplied by the Commissioner that there are reasonable grounds for suspecting—

(a)   that a data controller has contravened or is contravening any of the data protection principles, or

(b)   that an offence under this Act has been or is being committed,
and that evidence of the contravention or of the commission of the offence is to be found on any premises specified in the information, he may, subject to subparagraph (2) and paragraph 2, grant a warrant to the Commissioner.

(2)   A judge shall not issue a warrant under this Schedule in respect of any personal data processed for the special purposes unless a determination by the Commissioner under section 45 with respect to those data has taken effect.

(3)   A warrant issued under sub-paragraph (1) shall authorise the Commissioner or any of his officers or staff at any time within seven days of the date of the warrant to enter the premises, to search them, to inspect, examine, operate and test any equipment found there which is used or intended to be used for the processing of personal data and to inspect and seize any documents or other material found there which may be such evidence as is mentioned in that sub-paragraph.

2.—(1)   A judge shall not issue a warrant under this Schedule unless he is satisfied—

(a)   that the Commissioner has given seven days' notice in writing to the occupier of the premises in question demanding access to the premises, and

(b)   that either—

(i)   access was demanded at a reasonable hour and was unreasonably refused, or

(ii)   although entry to the premises was granted, the occupier unreasonably refused to comply with a request by the Commissioner or any of the Commissioner's officers or staff to permit the Commissioner or the officer or member of staff to do any of the things referred to in paragraph 1(3), and

(c)   that the occupier, has, after the refusal, been notified by the Commissioner of the application for the warrant and has had an opportunity of being heard by the judge on the question whether or not it should be issued.

(2)   Sub-paragraph (1) shall not apply if the judge is satisfied that the case is one of urgency or that compliance with those provisions would defeat the object of the entry.

3.   A judge who issues a warrant under this Schedule shall also issue two copies of it and certify them clearly as copies.

Execution of warrants

4.   A person executing a warrant issued under this Schedule may use such reasonable force as may be necessary.

5.   A warrant issued under this Schedule shall be executed at a reasonable hour unless it appears to the person executing it that there are grounds for suspecting that the evidence in question would not be found if it were so executed.

6.   If the person who occupies the premises in respect of which a warrant is issued under this Schedule is present when the warrant is executed, he shall be shown the warrant and supplied with a copy of it; and if that person is not present a copy of the warrant shall be left in a prominent place on the premises.

7.—(1)   A person seizing anything in pursuance of a warrant under this Schedule shall give a receipt for it if asked to do so.

(2)   Anything so seized may be retained for so long as is necessary in all the circumstances but the person in occupation of the premises in question shall be given a copy of anything that is seized if he so requests and the person executing the warrant considers that it can be done without undue delay.

Matters exempt from inspection and seizure

8.   The powers of inspection and seizure conferred by a warrant issued under this Schedule shall not be exercisable in respect of personal data which by virtue of section 28 are exempt from any of the provisions of this Act.

9.—(1)   Subject to the provisions of this paragraph, the powers of inspection and seizure conferred by a warrant issued under this Schedule shall not be exercisable in respect of—

(a)   any communication between a professional legal adviser and his client in connection with the giving of legal advice to the client with respect to his obligations, liabilities or rights under this Act, or

(b)   any communication between a professional legal adviser and his client, or between such an adviser or his client and any other person, made in connection with or in contemplation of proceedings under or arising out of this Act (including proceedings before the Tribunal) and for the purposes of such proceedings.

(2)   Sub-paragraph (1) applies also to—

(a)   any copy or other record of any such communication as is there mentioned, and

(b)   any document or article enclosed with or referred to in any such communication if made in connection with the giving of any advice or, as the case may be, in connection with or in contemplation of and for the purposes of such proceedings as are there mentioned.

(3)   This paragraph does not apply to anything in the possession of any person other than the professional legal adviser or his client or to anything held with the intention of furthering a criminal purpose.

(4)   In this paragraph references to the client of a professional legal adviser include references to any person representing such a client.

10.   If the person in occupation of any premises in respect of which a warrant is issued under this Schedule objects to the inspection or seizure under the warrant of any material on the grounds that it consists partly of matters in respect of which those powers are not exercisable, he shall, if the person executing the warrant so requests, furnish that person with a copy of so much of the material as is not exempt from those powers.

Return of warrants

11.   A warrant issued under this Schedule shall be returned to the court from which it was issued—
  (a)   after being executed, or
  (b)   if not executed within the time authorised for its execution;
and the person by whom any such warrant is executed shall make an endorsement on it stating what powers have been exercised by him under the warrant.

Offences

12.   Any person who—
  (a)   intentionally obstructs a person in the execution of a warrant issued under this Schedule, or
  (b)   fails without reasonable excuse to give any person executing such a warrant such assistance as he may reasonably require for the execution of the warrant, is guilty of an offence.

Vessels, vehicles etc.

13.   In this Schedule 'premises' includes any vessel, vehicle, aircraft or hovercraft, and references to the occupier of any premises include references to the person in charge of any vessel, vehicle, aircraft or hovercraft.

Scotland and Northern Ireland

14.   In the application of this Schedule to Scotland—
  (a)   for any reference to a circuit judge there is substituted a reference to the sheriff,
  (b)   for any reference to information on oath there is substituted a reference to evidence on oath, and
  (c)   for the reference to the court from which the warrant was issued there is substituted a reference to the sheriff clerk.

15.   In the application of this Schedule to Northern Ireland—
  (a)   for any reference to a circuit judge there is substituted a reference to a county court judge, and
  (b)   for any reference to information on oath there is substituted a reference to a complaint on oath.

Section 53(6)   SCHEDULE 10
                    FURTHER PROVISIONS RELATING TO ASSISTANCE
                    UNDER SECTION 53

1.   In this Schedule 'applicant' and 'proceedings' have the same meaning as in section 53.

2.   The assistance provided under section 53 may include the making of arrangements for, or for the Commissioner to bear the costs of—

(a)   the giving of advice or assistance by a solicitor or counsel, and

(b)   the representation of the applicant, or the provision to him of such assistance as is usually given by a solicitor or counsel—

(i)   in steps preliminary or incidental to the proceedings, or

(ii)   in arriving at or giving effect to a compromise to avoid or bring an end to the proceedings.

3.   Where assistance is provided with respect to the conduct of proceedings—

(a)   it shall include an agreement by the Commissioner to indemnify the applicant (subject only to any exceptions specified in the notification) in respect of any liability to pay costs or expenses arising by virtue of any judgment or order of the court in the proceedings,

(b)   it may include an agreement by the Commissioner to indemnify the applicant in respect of any liability to pay costs or expenses arising by virtue of any compromise or settlement arrived at in order to avoid the proceedings or bring the proceedings to an end, and

(c)   it may include an agreement by the Commissioner to indemnify the applicant in respect of any liability to pay damages pursuant to an undertaking given on the grant of interlocutory relief (in Scotland, an interim order) to the applicant.

4.   Where the Commissioner provides assistance in relation to any proceedings, he shall do so on such terms, or make such other arrangements, as will secure that a person against whom the proceedings have been or are commenced is informed that assistance has been or is being provided by the Commissioner in relation to them.

5.   In England and Wales or Northern Ireland, the recovery of expenses incurred by the Commissioner in providing an applicant with assistance (as taxed or assessed in such manner as may be prescribed by rules of court) shall constitute a first charge for the benefit of the Commissioner—

(a)   on any costs which, by virtue of any judgment or order of the court, are payable to the applicant by any other person in respect of the matter in connection with which the assistance is provided, and

(b)   on any sum payable to the applicant under a compromise or settlement arrived at in connection with that matter to avoid or bring to an end any proceedings.

6.   In Scotland, the recovery of such expenses (as taxed or assessed in such manner as may be prescribed by rules of court) shall be paid to the Commissioner, in priority to other debts—

(a)   out of any expenses which, by virtue of any judgment or order of the court, are payable to the applicant by any other person in respect of the matter in connection with which the assistance is provided, and

(b)   out of any sum payable to the applicant under a compromise or settlement arrived at in connection with that matter to avoid or bring to an end any proceedings.

Section 68(1)(6)   SCHEDULE 11
                              EDUCATIONAL RECORDS

Meaning of 'educational record'

1.   For the purposes of section 68 'educational record' means any record to which paragraph 2, 5 or 7 applies.

England and Wales

2.   This paragraph applies to any record of information which—
    (a)   is processed by or on behalf of the governing body of, or a teacher at, any school in England and Wales specified in paragraph 3,
    (b)   relates to any person who is or has been a pupil at the school, and
    (c)   originated from or was supplied by or on behalf of any of the persons specified in paragraph 4,
other than information which is processed by a teacher solely for the teacher's own use.

3.   The schools referred to in paragraph 2(a) are—
    (a)   a school maintained by a local education authority, and
    (b)   a special school, as defined by section 6(2) of the Education Act 1996, which is not so maintained.

4.   The persons referred to in paragraph 2(c) are—
    (a)   an employee of the local education authority which maintains the school,
    (b)   in the case of—
        (i)   a voluntary aided, foundation or foundation special school (within the meaning of the School Standards and Framework Act 1998), or
        (ii)   a special school which is not maintained by a local education authority, a teacher or other employee at the school (including an educational psychologist engaged by the governing body under a contract for services),
    (c)   the pupil to whom the record relates, and
    (d)   a parent, as defined by section 576(1) of the Education Act 1996, of that pupil.

Scotland

5.   This paragraph applies to any record of information which is processed—
    (a)   by an education authority in Scotland, and
    (b)   for the purpose of the relevant function of the authority,
other than information which is processed by a teacher solely for the teacher's own use.

6.   For the purposes of paragraph 5—
    (a)   'education authority' means an education authority within the meaning of the Education (Scotland) Act 1980 ('the 1980 Act') or, in relation to a self-governing school, the board of management within the meaning of the Self-Governing Schools etc. (Scotland) Act 1989 ('the 1989 Act'),
    (b)   'the relevant function' means, in relation to each of those authorities, their function under section 1 of the 1980 Act and section 7(1) of the 1989 Act, and
    (c)   information processed by an education authority is processed for the purpose of the relevant function of the authority if the processing relates to the discharge of that function in respect of a person—

(i)   who is or has been a pupil in a school provided by the authority, or

(ii)   who receives, or has received, further education (within the meaning of the 1980 Act) so provided.

Northern Ireland

7.—(1)   This paragraph applies to any record of information which—

(a)   is processed by or on behalf of the Board of Governors of, or a teacher at, any grant-aided school in Northern Ireland,

(b)   relates to any person who is or has been a pupil at the school, and

(c)   originated from or was supplied by or on behalf of any of the persons specified in paragraph 8,

other than information which is processed by a teacher solely for the teacher's own use.

(2)   In sub-paragraph (1) 'grant-aided school' has the same meaning as in the Education and Libraries (Northern Ireland) Order 1986.

8.   The persons referred to in paragraph 7(1) are—

(a)   a teacher at the school,

(b)   an employee of an education and library board, other than such a teacher,

(c)   the pupil to whom the record relates, and

(d)   a parent (as defined by Article 2(2) of the Education and Libraries (Northern Ireland) Order 1986) of that pupil.

England and Wales: transitory provisions

9.—(1)   Until the appointed day within the meaning of section 20 of the School Standards and Framework Act 1998, this Schedule shall have effect subject to the following modifications.

(2)   Paragraph 3 shall have effect as if for paragraph (b) and the 'and' immediately preceding it there were substituted—

'(aa)   a grant-maintained school, as defined by section 183(1) of the Education Act 1996,

(ab)   a grant-maintained special school, as defined by section 337(4) of that Act, and

(b)   a special school, as defined by section 6(2) of that Act, which is neither a maintained special school, as defined by section 337(3) of that Act, nor a grant-maintained special school.'

(3)   Paragraph 4(b)(i) shall have effect as if for the words from 'foundation', in the first place where it occurs, to '1998)' there were substituted 'or grant-maintained school'.

Section 68(1)(c)   SCHEDULE 12
                        ACCESSIBLE PUBLIC RECORDS

Meaning of 'accessible public record'

1.   For the purposes of section 68 'accessible public record' means any record which is kept by an authority specified—

(a)   as respects England and Wales, in the Table in paragraph 2,

(b)   as respects Scotland, in the Table in paragraph 4, or

(c)   as respects Northern Ireland, in the Table in paragraph 6,

and is a record of information of a description specified in that Table in relation to that authority.

Housing and social services records: England and Wales

2.   The following is the Table referred to in paragraph 1(a).

TABLE OF AUTHORITIES AND INFORMATION

The authorities	*The accessible information*
Housing Act local authority.	Information held for the purpose of any of the authority's tenancies.
Local social services authority.	Information held for any purpose of the authority's social services functions.

3.—(1)   The following provisions apply for the interpretation of the Table in paragraph 2.

(2)   Any authority which, by virtue of section 4(e) of the Housing Act 1985, is a local authority for the purpose of any provision of that Act is a 'Housing Act local authority' for the purposes of this Schedule, and so is any housing action trust established under Part III of the Housing Act 1988.

(3)   Information contained in records kept by a Housing Act local authority is 'held for the purpose of any of the authority's tenancies' if it is held for any purpose of the relationship of landlord and tenant of a dwelling which subsists, has subsisted or may subsist between the authority and any individual who is, has been or, as the case may be, has applied to be, a tenant of the authority.

(4)   Any authority which, by virtue of section 1 or 12 of the Local Authority Social Services Act 1970, is or is treated as a local authority for the purposes of that Act is a 'local social services authority' for the purposes of this Schedule; and information contained in records kept by such an authority is 'held for any purpose of the authority's social services functions' if it is held for the purpose of any past, current or proposed exercise of such a function in any case.

(5)   Any expression used in paragraph 2 or this paragraph and in Part II of the Housing Act 1985 or the Local Authority Social Services Act 1970 has the same meaning as in that Act.

Housing and social services records: Scotland

4.   The following is the Table referred to in paragraph 1(b).

TABLE OF AUTHORITIES AND INFORMATION

The authorities	The accessible information
Local authority. Scottish Homes.	Information held for the purpose of any of the body's tenancies.
Social work authority.	Information held for any purpose of the the authority's functions under the Social Work (Scotland) Act 1968 and the enactments referred to in section 5(1B) of that Act.

5.—(1) The following provisions apply for the interpretation of the Table in paragraph 4.

(2) 'Local authority' means—

(a) a council constituted under section 2 of the Local Government etc. (Scotland) Act 1994,

(b) a joint board or joint committee of two or more of those councils, or

(c) any trust under the control of such a council.

(3) Information contained in records kept by a local authority or Scottish Homes is held for the purpose of any of their tenancies if it is held for any purpose of the relationship of landlord and tenant of a dwelling-house which subsists, has subsisted or may subsist between the authority or, as the case may be, Scottish Homes and any individual who is, has been or, as the case may be, has applied to be a tenant of theirs.

(4) 'Social work authority' means a local authority for the purposes of the Social Work (Scotland) Act 1968, and information contained in records kept by such an authority is held for any purpose of their functions if it is held for the purpose of any past, current or proposed exercise of such a function in any case.

Housing and social services records: Northern Ireland

6.   The following is the Table referred to in paragraph 1(c).

TABLE OF AUTHORITIES AND INFORMATION

The authorities	The accessible information
The Northern Ireland Housing Executive.	Information held for the purpose of any of the Executive's tenancies.
A Health and Social Services Board.	Information held for the purpose of any past, current or proposed exercise by the Board of any function exercisable, by virtue of directions under Article 17(1) of the Health and Personal Social Services (Northern Ireland) Order 1972, by the Board on behalf of the Department of Health and Social Services with respect to the administration of personal social services under—

The authorities	The accessible information
	(a) the Children and Young Persons Act (Northern Ireland) 1968; (b) the Health and Personal Social Services (Northern Ireland) Order 1972; (c) Article 47 of the Matrimonial Causes (Northern Ireland) Order 1978; (d) Article 11 of the Domestic Proceedings (Northern Ireland) Order 1980; (e) the Adoption (Northern Ireland) Order 1987; or (f) the Children (Northern Ireland) Order 1995.
An HSS trust	Information held for the purpose of any past, current or proposed exercise by the trust of any function exercisable, by virtue of an authorisation under Article 3(1) of the Health and Personal Social Services (Northern Ireland) Order 1994, by the trust on behalf of a Health and Social Services Board with respect to the administration of personal social services under any statutory provision mentioned in the last preceding entry.

7.—(1) This paragraph applies for the interpretation of the Table in paragraph 6.

(2) Information contained in records kept by the Northern Ireland Housing Executive is 'held for the purpose of any of the Executive's tenancies' if it is held for any purpose of the relationship of landlord and tenant of a dwelling which subsists, has subsisted or may subsist between the Executive and any individual who is, has been or, as the case may be, has applied to be, a tenant of the Executive.

Section 72   SCHEDULE 13
MODIFICATIONS OF ACT HAVING EFFECT BEFORE
24TH OCTOBER 2007

1. After section 12 there is inserted—

'12A. Rights of data subjects in relation to exempt manual data
(1) A data subject is entitled at any time by notice in writing—
    (a) to require the data controller to rectify, block, erase or destroy exempt manual data which are inaccurate or incomplete, or
    (b) to require the data controller to cease holding exempt manual data in a way incompatible with the legitimate purposes pursued by the data controller.

(2)   A notice under subsection (1)(a) or (b) must state the data subject's reasons for believing that the data are inaccurate or incomplete or, as the case may be, his reasons for believing that they are held in a way incompatible with the legitimate purposes pursued by the data controller.

(3)   If the court is satisfied, on the application of any person who has given a notice under subsection (1) which appears to the court to be justified (or to be justified to any extent) that the data controller in question has failed to comply with the notice, the court may order him to take such steps for complying with the notice (or for complying with it to that extent) as the court thinks fit.

(4)   In this section 'exempt manual data' means—

(a)   in relation to the first transitional period, as defined by paragraph 1(2) of Schedule 8, data to which paragraph 3 or 4 of that Schedule applies, and

(b)   in relation to the second transitional period, as so defined, data to which paragraph 14 of that Schedule applies.

(5)   For the purposes of this section personal data are incomplete if, and only if, the data, although not inaccurate, are such that their incompleteness would constitute a contravention of the third or fourth data protection principles, if those principles applied to the data.'

2.   In section 32—

(a)   in subsection (2) after 'section 12' there is inserted—

'(dd) section 12A,', and

(b)   in subsection (4) after '12(8)' there is inserted ', 12A(3)'.

3.   In section 34 for 'section 14(1) to (3)' there is substituted 'sections 12A and 14(1) to (3).'

4.   In section 53(1) after '12(8)' there is inserted ', 12A(3)'.

5.   In paragraph 8 of Part II of Schedule 1, the word 'or' at the end of paragraph (c) is omitted and after paragraph (d) there is inserted 'or

(e)   he contravenes section 12A by failing to comply with a notice given under subsection (1) of that section to the extent that the notice is justified.'

Section 73   SCHEDULE 14
                    TRANSITIONAL PROVISIONS AND SAVINGS

Interpretation

1.   In this Schedule—

'the 1984 Act' means the Data Protection Act 1984;

'the old principles' means the data protection principles within the meaning of the 1984 Act;

'the new principles' means the data protection principles within the meaning of this Act.

Effect of registration under Part II of 1984 Act

2.—(1)   Subject to sub-paragraphs (4) and (5) any person who, immediately before the commencement of Part III of this Act—

(a)   is registered as a data user under Part II of the 1984 Act, or

(b)   is treated by virtue of section 7(6) of the 1984 Act as so registered, is exempt from section 17(1) of this Act until the end of the registration period or, if earlier, 24th October 2001.

(2)   In sub-paragraph (1) 'the registration period', in relation to a person, means—

(a)   where there is a single entry in respect of that person as a data user, the period at the end of which, if section 8 of the 1984 Act had remained in force, that entry would have fallen to be removed unless renewed, and

(b)   where there are two or more entries in respect of that person as a data user, the period at the end of which, if that section had remained in force, the last of those entries to expire would have fallen to be removed unless renewed.

(3)   Any application for registration as a data user under Part II of the 1984 Act which is received by the Commissioner before the commencement of Part III of this Act (including any appeal against a refusal of registration) shall be determined in accordance with the old principles and the provisions of the 1984 Act.

(4)   If a person falling within paragraph (b) of sub-paragraph (1) receives a notification under section 7(1) of the 1984 Act of the refusal of his application, sub-paragraph (1) shall cease to apply to him—

(a)   if no appeal is brought, at the end of the period within which an appeal can be brought against the refusal, or

(b)   on the withdrawal or dismissal of the appeal.

(5)   If a data controller gives a notification under section 18(1) at a time when he is exempt from section 17(1) by virtue of sub-paragraph (1), he shall cease to be so exempt.

(6)   The Commissioner shall include in the register maintained under section 19 an entry in respect of each person who is exempt from section 17(1) by virtue of sub-paragraph (1); and each entry shall consist of the particulars which, immediately before the commencement of Part III of this Act, were included (or treated as included) in respect of that person in the register maintained under section 4 of the 1984 Act.

(7)   Notification regulations under Part III of this Act may make provision modifying the duty referred to in section 20(1) in its application to any person in respect of whom an entry in the register maintained under section 19 has been made under sub-paragraph (6).

(8)   Notification regulations under Part III of this Act may make further transitional provision in connection with the substitution of Part III of this Act for Part II of the 1984 Act (registration), including provision modifying the application of provisions of Part III in transitional cases.

Rights of data subjects

3.—(1)   The repeal of section 21 of the 1984 Act (right of access to personal data) does not affect the application of that section in any case in which the request (together with the information referred to in paragraph (a) of subsection (4) of that section and, in a case where it is required, the consent referred to in paragraph (b) of that subsection) was received before the day on which the repeal comes into force.

(2)   Sub-paragraph (1) does not apply where the request is made by reference to this Act.

(3)   Any fee paid for the purposes of section 21 of the 1984 Act before the commencement of section 7 in a case not falling within sub-paragraph (1) shall be taken to have been paid for the purposes of section 7.

4.   The repeal of section 22 of the 1984 Act (compensation for inaccuracy) and the repeal of section 23 of that Act (compensation for loss or unauthorised disclosure) do not affect the application of those sections in relation to damage or distress suffered at any time by reason of anything done or omitted to be done before the commencement of the repeals.

5.   The repeal of section 24 of the 1984 Act (rectification and erasure) does not affect any case in which the application to the court was made before the day on which the repeal comes into force.

6.   Subsection (3)(b) of section 14 does not apply where the rectification, blocking, erasure or destruction occurred before the commencement of that section.

Enforcement and transfer prohibition notices served under Part V of 1984 Act

7.—(1)   If, immediately before the commencement of section 40—

(a)   an enforcement notice under section 10 of the 1984 Act has effect, and

(b)   either the time for appealing against the notice has expired or any appeal has been determined,

then, after that commencement, to the extent mentioned in sub-paragraph (3), the notice shall have effect for the purposes of sections 41 and 47 as if it were an enforcement notice under section 40.

(2)   Where an enforcement notice has been served under section 10 of the 1984 Act before the commencement of section 40 and immediately before that commencement either—

(a)   the time for appealing against the notice has not expired, or

(b)   an appeal has not been determined,

the appeal shall be determined in accordance with the provisions of the 1984 Act and the old principles and, unless the notice is quashed on appeal, to the extent mentioned in sub-paragraph (3) the notice shall have effect for the purposes of sections 41 and 47 as if it were an enforcement notice under section 40.

(3)   An enforcement notice under section 10 of the 1984 Act has the effect described in sub-paragraph (1) or (2) only to the extent that the steps specified in the notice for complying with the old principle or principles in question are steps which the data controller could be required by an enforcement notice under section 40 to take for complying with the new principles or any of them.

8.—(1)   If, immediately before the commencement of section 40—

(a)   a transfer prohibition notice under section 12 of the 1984 Act has effect, and

(b)   either the time for appealing against the notice has expired or any appeal has been determined,

then, on and after that commencement, to the extent specified in sub-paragraph (3), the notice shall have effect for the purposes of sections 41 and 47 as if it were an enforcement notice under section 40.

(2)   Where a transfer prohibition notice has been served under section 12 of the 1984 Act and immediately before the commencement of section 40 either—

(a)   the time for appealing against the notice has not expired, or

(b)   an appeal has not been determined,

the appeal shall be determined in accordance with the provisions of the 1984 Act and the old principles and, unless the notice is quashed on appeal, to the extent mentioned in sub-paragraph (3) the notice shall have effect for the purposes of sections 41 and 47 as if it were an enforcement notice under section 40.

(3)   A transfer prohibition notice under section 12 of the 1984 Act has the effect described in sub-paragraph (1) or (2) only to the extent that the prohibition imposed by the notice is one which could be imposed by an enforcement notice under section 40 for complying with the new principles or any of them.

Notices under new law relating to matters in relation to which 1984 Act had effect

9.   The Commissioner may serve an enforcement notice under section 40 on or after the day on which that section comes into force if he is satisfied that, before that day, the data controller contravened the old principles by reason of any act or omission which would also have constituted a contravention of the new principles if they had applied before that day.

10.   Subsection (5)(b) of section 40 does not apply where the rectification, blocking, erasure or destruction occurred before the commencement of that section.

11.   The Commissioner may serve an information notice under section 43 on or after the day on which that section comes into force if he has reasonable grounds for suspecting that, before that day, the data controller contravened the old principles by reason of any act or omission which would also have constituted a contravention of the new principles if they had applied before that day.

12.   Where by virtue of paragraph 11 an information notice is served on the basis of anything done or omitted to be done before the day on which section 43 comes into force, subsection (2)(b) of that section shall have effect as if the reference to the data controller having complied, or complying, with the new principles were a reference to the data controller having contravened the old principles by reason of any such act or omission as is mentioned in paragraph 11.

Self-incrimination, etc.

13.—(1)   In section 43(8), section 44(9) and paragraph 11 of Schedule 7, any reference to an offence under this Act includes a reference to an offence under the 1984 Act.

(2)   In section 34(9) of the 1984 Act, any reference to an offence under that Act includes a reference to an offence under this Act.

Warrants issued under 1984 Act

14.   The repeal of Schedule 4 to the 1984 Act does not affect the application of that Schedule in any case where a warrant was issued under that Schedule before the commencement of the repeal.

Complaints under section 36(2) of 1984 Act and requests for assessment under section 42

15.   The repeal of section 36(2) of the 1984 Act does not affect the application of that provision in any case where the complaint was received by the Commissioner before the commencement of the repeal.

16.   In dealing with a complaint under section 36(2) of the 1984 Act or a request for an assessment under section 42 of this Act, the Commissioner shall have regard to the provisions from time to time applicable to the processing, and accordingly—

(a)   in section 36(2) of the 1984 Act, the reference to the old principles and the provisions of that Act includes, in relation to any time when the new principles and the provisions of this Act have effect, those principles and provisions, and

(b)   in section 42 of this Act, the reference to the provisions of this Act includes, in relation to any time when the old principles and the provisions of the 1984 Act had effect, those principles and provisions.

Applications under Access to Health Records Act 1990 or corresponding Northern Ireland legislation

17.—(1)   The repeal of any provision of the Access to Health Records Act 1990 does not affect—

(a)   the application of section 3 or 6 of that Act in any case in which the application under that section was received before the day on which the repeal comes into force, or

(b)   the application of section 8 of that Act in any case in which the application to the court was made before the day on which the repeal comes into force.

(2)   Sub-paragraph (1)(a) does not apply in relation to an application for access to information which was made by reference to this Act.

18.—(1)   The revocation of any provision of the Access to Health Records (Northern Ireland) Order 1993 does not affect—

(a)   the application of Article 5 or 8 of that Order in any case in which the application under that Article was received before the day on which the repeal comes into force, or

(b)   the application of Article 10 of that Order in any case in which the application to the court was made before the day on which the repeal comes into force.

(2)   Sub-paragraph (1)(a) does not apply in relation to an application for access to information which was made by reference to this Act.

Applications under regulations under Access to Personal Files Act 1987 or corresponding Northern Ireland legislation

19.—(1)   The repeal of the personal files enactments does not affect the application of regulations under those enactments in relation to—

(a)   any request for information,

(b)   any application for rectification or erasure, or

(c)   any application for review of a decision,

which was made before the day on which the repeal comes into force.

(2)   Sub-paragraph (1)(a) does not apply in relation to a request for information which was made by reference to this Act.

(3)   In sub-paragraph (1) 'the personal files enactments' means—

(a)   in relation to Great Britain, the Access to Personal Files Act 1987, and

(b)   in relation to Northern Ireland, Part II of the Access to Personal Files and Medical Reports (Northern Ireland) Order 1991.

Applications under section 158 of Consumer Credit Act 1974

20.   Section 62 does not affect the application of section 158 of the Consumer Credit Act 1974 in any case where the request was received before the commencement of section 62, unless the request is made by reference to this Act.

Section 74(1)   SCHEDULE 15
                   MINOR AND CONSEQUENTIAL AMENDMENTS

Public Records Act 1958 (c. 51)

1.—(1)   In Part II of the Table in paragraph 3 of Schedule 1 to the Public Records
Act 1958 (definition of public records) for 'the Data Protection Registrar' there is
substituted 'the Data Protection Commissioner'.

(2)   That Schedule shall continue to have effect with the following amendment
(originally made by paragraph 14 of Schedule 2 to the Data Protection Act 1984).

(3)   After paragraph 4(1)(n) there is inserted—

'(nn) records of the Data Protection Tribunal'.

Parliamentary Commissioner Act 1967 (c. 13)

2.   In Schedule 2 to the Parliamentary Commissioner Act 1967 (departments etc.
subject to investigation) for 'Data Protection Registrar' there is substituted 'Data
Protection Commissioner'.

3.   In Schedule 4 to that Act (tribunals exercising administrative functions), in the
entry relating to the Data Protection Tribunal, for 'section 3 of the Data Protection
Act 1984' there is substituted 'section 6 of the Data Protection Act 1998'.

Superannuation Act 1972 (c. 11)

4.   In Schedule 1 to the Superannuation Act 1972, for 'Data Protection Registrar'
there is substituted 'Data Protection Commissioner'.

House of Commons Disqualification Act 1975 (c. 24)

5.—(1)   Part II of Schedule 1 to the House of Commons Disqualification Act 1975
(bodies whose members are disqualified) shall continue to include the entry 'The Data
Protection Tribunal' (originally inserted by paragraph 12(1) of Schedule 2 to the Data
Protection Act 1984).

(2)   In Part III of that Schedule (disqualifying offices) for 'The Data Protection
Registrar' there is substituted 'The Data Protection Commissioner'.

Northern Ireland Assembly Disqualification Act 1975 (c. 25)

6.—(1)   Part II of Schedule 1 to the Northern Ireland Assembly Disqualification
Act 1975 (bodies whose members are disqualified) shall continue to include the entry
'The Data Protection Tribunal' (originally inserted by paragraph 12(3) of Schedule 2
to the Data Protection Act 1984).

(2)   In Part III of that Schedule (disqualifying offices) for 'The Data Protection
Registrar' there is substituted 'The Data Protection Commissioner'.

Representation of the People Act 1983 (c. 2)

7.   In Schedule 2 of the Representation of the People Act 1983 (provisions which
may be included in regulations as to registration etc), in paragraph 11A(2)—

(a)   for 'data user' there is substituted 'data controller' and

(b)   for 'the Data Protection Act 1984' there is substituted 'the Data Protection
Act 1998'.

Access to Medical Reports Act 1988 (c. 28)

8.   In section 2(1) of the Access to Medical Reports Act 1988 (interpretation), in the definition of 'health professional', for 'the Data Protection (Subject Access Modification) Order 1987' there is substituted 'the Data Protection Act 1998'.

Football Spectators Act 1989 (c. 37)

9.—(1)   Section 5 of the Football Spectators Act 1989 (national membership scheme: contents and penalties) is amended as follows.

(2)   In subsection (5), for 'paragraph 1(2) of Part II of Schedule 1 to the Data Protection Act 1984' there is substituted 'paragraph 1(2) of Part II of Schedule 1 to the Data Protection Act 1998'.

(3)   In subsection (6), for 'section 28(1) and (2) of the Data Protection Act 1984' there is substituted 'section 29(1) and (2) of the Data Protection Act 1998'.

Education (Student Loans) Act 1990 (c. 6)

10.   Schedule 2 to the Education (Student Loans) Act 1990 (loans for students) so far as that Schedule continues in force shall have effect as if the reference in paragraph 4(2) to the Data Protection Act 1984 were a reference to this Act.

Access to Health Records Act 1990 (c. 23)

11.   For section 2 of the Access to Health Records Act 1990 there is substituted—

'2.   Health professionals
In this Act 'health professional' has the same meaning as in the Data Protection Act 1998.'

12.   In section 3(4) of that Act (cases where fee may be required) in paragraph (a), for 'the maximum prescribed under section 21 of the Data Protection Act 1984' there is substituted 'such maximum as may be prescribed for the purposes of this section by regulations under section 7 of the Data Protection Act 1998'.

13.   In section 5(3) of that Act (cases where right of access may be partially excluded) for the words from the beginning to 'record' in the first place where it occurs there is substituted 'Access shall not be given under section 3(2) to any part of a health record'.

Access to Personal Files and Medical Reports (Northern Ireland) Order 1991 (1991/1707 (N.I. 14))

14.   In Article 4 of the Access to Personal Files and Medical Reports (Northern Ireland) Order 1991 (obligation to give access), in paragraph (2) (exclusion of information to which individual entitled under section 21 of the Data Protection Act 1984) for 'section 21 of the Data Protection Act 1984' there is substituted 'section 7 of the Data Protection Act 1998'.

15.   In Article 6(1) of that Order (interpretation), in the definition of 'health professional', for 'the Data Protection (Subject Access Modification) (Health) Order 1987' there is substituted 'the Data Protection Act 1998'.

Tribunals and Inquiries Act 1992 (c. 53)

16.   In Part 1 of Schedule 1 to the Tribunals and Inquiries Act 1992 (tribunals under direct supervision of Council on Tribunals), for paragraph 14 there is substituted—

'Data protection

14(a) The Data Protection Commissioner appointed under section 6 of the Data Protection Act 1998;

(b)   the Data Protection Tribunal constituted under that section, in respect of its jurisdiction under section 48 of that Act.'

Access to Health Records (Northern Ireland) Order 1993 (1993/1250 (N.I. 4))

17.   For paragraphs (1) and (2) of Article 4 of the Access to Health Records (Northern Ireland) Order 1993 there is substituted—

'(1)   In this Order ''health professional'' has the same meaning as in the Data Protection Act 1998.'

18.   In Article 5(4) of that Order (cases where fee may be required) in sub-paragraph (a), for 'the maximum prescribed under section 21 of the Data Protection Act 1984' there is substituted 'such maximum as may be prescribed for the purposes of this Article by regulations under section 7 of the Data Protection Act 1998'.

19.   In Article 7 of that Order (cases where right of access may be partially excluded) for the words from the beginning to 'record' in the first place where it occurs there is substituted 'Access shall not be given under Article 5(2) to any part of a health record'.

Section 74(2)   SCHEDULE 16
REPEALS AND REVOCATIONS

PART I
REPEALS

Chapter	Short title	Extent of repeal
1984 c. 35.	The Data Protection Act 1984.	The whole Act.
1986 c. 60.	The Financial Services Act 1986.	Section 190.
1987 c. 37.	The Access to Personal Files Act 1987.	The whole Act.
1988 c. 40.	The Education Reform Act 1988.	Section 223.
1988 c. 50.	The Housing Act 1988.	In Schedule 17, paragraph 80.
1990 c. 23.	The Access to Health Records Act 1990.	In section 1(1), the words from 'but does not' to the end.

Chapter	Short title	Extent of repeal
		In section 3, subsection (1)(a) to (e) and, in subsection (6)(a), the words 'in the case of an application made otherwise than by the patient'. Section 4(1) and (2). In section 5(1)(a)(i), the words 'of the patient or' and the word 'other'. In section 10, in sub-section (2) the words 'or orders' and in subsection (3) the words 'or an order under section 2(3) above'. In section 11, the definitions of 'child' and 'parental responsibility'.
1990 c. 37.	The Human Fertilisation and Embryology Act 1990.	Section 33(8).
1990 c. 41.	The Courts and Legal Services Act 1990.	In Schedule 10, paragraph 58.
1992 c. 13.	The Further and Higher Education Act 1992.	Section 86.
1992 c. 37.	The Further and Higher Education (Scotland) Act 1992.	Section 59.
1993 c. 8.	The Judicial Pensions and Retirement Act 1993.	In Schedule 6, paragraph 50.
1993 c. 10.	The Charities Act 1993.	Section 12.
1993 c. 21.	The Osteopaths Act 1993.	Section 38.
1994 c. 17.	The Chiropractors Act 1994.	Section 38.
1994 c. 19.	The Local Government (Wales) Act 1994.	In Schedule 13, paragraph 30.
1994 c. 33.	The Criminal Justice and Public Order Act 1994.	Section 161.
1994 c. 39.	The Local Government (Scotland) Act 1994.	In Schedule 13, paragraph 154.

PART II
REVOCATIONS

Number	Title	Extent of revocation
S.I. 1991/1142.	The Data Protection Registration Fee Order 1991.	The whole Order.
S.I. 1991/1707 (N.I. 14).	The Access to Personal Files and Medical Reports (Northern Ireland) Order 1991.	Part II. The Schedule.
S.I. 1992/3218.	The Banking Co-ordination (Second Council Directive) Regulations 1992.	In Schedule 10, paragraphs 15 and 40.
S.I. 1993/1250 (N.I. 4).	The Access to Health Records (Northern Ireland) Order 1993.	In Article 2(2), the definitions of 'child' and 'parental responsibility'. In Article 3(1), the words from 'but does not include' to the end. In Article 5, paragraph (1)(a) to (d) and, in paragraph (6)(a), the words 'in the case of an application made otherwise than by the patient'. Article 6(1) and (2). In Article 7(1)(a)(i), the words 'of the patient or' and the word 'other'.
S.I. 1994/429 (N.I. 2).	The Health and Personal Social Services (Northern Ireland) Order 1994.	In Schedule 1, the entries relating to the Access to Personal Files and Medical Reports (Northern Ireland) Order 1991.
S.I. 1994/1696.	The Insurance Companies (Third Insurance Directives) Regulations 1994.	In Schedule 8, paragraph 8.
S.I. 1995/755 (N.I. 2).	The Children (Northern Ireland) Order 1995.	In Schedule 9, paragraphs 177 and 191.

Number	Title	Extent of revocation
S.I. 1995/3275.	The Investment Services Regulations 1995.	In Schedule 10, paragraphs 3 and 15.
S.I. 1996/2827.	The Open-Ended Investment Companies (Investment Companies with Variable Capital) Regulations 1996.	In Schedule 8, paragraphs 3 and 26.

Index